CONQUERED, NOT DEFEATED

Growing Up in Denmark During the German Occupation of World War II

Peter H. Tveskov

Hellgate Press
Central Point, Oregon

Conquered, Not Defeated

Hellgate Press
An Imprint of PSI Research
P.O. Box 3727
Central Point, Oregon 97502

info@psi-research.com

Editing: Zanne Miller
Cover design: Michael Tveskov
Book design: Harley B. Patrick
Photo prep & map: Mark Tveskov

Library of Congress Cataloging-in-Publication Data

Tveskov, Peter H. , 1934-
   Conquered, not defeated : growing up in Denmark during the German
occupation of World War Two / Peter H. Tveskov.-- 1st ed.
        p. cm.
Includes bibliographical references .
   ISBN 1-55571-638-5 (pbk.)
1.   Tveskov, Peter H., 1934- 2.   World War, 1939-1945--Denmark. 3.
Denmark—History--German occupation, 1940-1945. 4.   World War,
1939-1945--Personal narratives, Danish.   I. Title.
   D802.D4T84 2003
940.53 ' 489 ' 092--dc22

                           2003015586

Printed and bound in the United States of America
First Edition 10 9 8 7 6 5 4 3 2 1

Cover photo: Summer 1943. The author, age 8 (left), and his cousin, Jan, age 9, on Venøgade Street, Copenhagen.

To my granddaughters—

Laura, Julia, and Clio:

May you never hear the order

"Ausweiss, bitte!" from anyone.

About the Author

Peter Tveskov was born in Copenhagen, Denmark, and lived there until three days after his fourteenth birthday in 1948, when he and his mother moved to Venezuela where he completed his secondary education. After returning to the States, he studied Mechanical Engineering at Yale University and earned the degree of Bachelor of Engineering in 1956.

Following ten years working in the oil fields of West Texas, Venezuela, and Brazil, he became the physical plant manager first at Yale University and later at Wesleyan University in Middletown, Connecticut. Later in his career, he served as a consultant in facilities operations that took him to assignments at Brown University, Connecticut College, Milton Academy, Vassar College, Choate Rosemary Hall, Monmouth College, Bryn Mawr College, and the Ethical Culture School in Manhattan. He retired in 1997.

Though retired, Mr. Tveskov continues working as a consultant in capital project management, as well as on assignments as a group leader for Elderhostel-Scandinavian Seminar, guiding groups of interesting and engaged senior citizens on tours of the three Scandinavian countries.

Peter Tveskov and his wife of 47 years, Judith, now live in the Short Beach section of Branford, Connecticut. They have four grown children and three grandchildren.

Contents

Illustrations

Photos (except #1, #2b, #3) originally appeared in "5 Years: The Occupation of Denmark in Pictures," Ernst Mentze; A.B. Allhems Förlag, Malmö, Sweden. Used with permission.

Introduction

Over the years I have shared my memories of my childhood in Denmark with my family and with other more or less interested friends, acquaintances and strangers. A number of people have suggested that I write down these recollections, but until my retirement in 1996 the opportunity never really presented itself. Once I began collecting these memories and impressions I also began studying the modern history of Denmark and the other Scandinavian countries and was surprised to find how many of my own memories tie in with documented events of the war years. Perhaps my observations will be of special interest to folks of my generation who shared these events.

One important source of this history has been Professor Byron J. Nordstrom's book, *Scandinavia Since 1500*, which provided a comprehensive background for the events that led up to the Second World War as it related to the Scandinavian countries. To me the most important aspect of Professor Nordstrom's book was that it presented an objective view of the histories of the three countries without the subjective interpretations I was taught in school in Denmark or the diverse subjective versions of the same historical events that I am sure were taught to my contemporaries in Sweden and Norway.

Following my retirement I also had the opportunity, on four separate occasions, to visit the Scandinavian countries as a group leader for Scandinavian Seminar, an Elderhostel program. During these trips I not only got to lead a group of interesting and engaged American senior citizens through programs on history and culture in the three countries, but also for the first time to visit areas in all three countries that I never had visited before. All these areas had historical connotations that for the first time became real for me.

For example, Denmark's loss of the Norwegian Bohuslen to Sweden in the sixteenth century had always been a minor historical footnote to Danish high school students, but to stand on the ramparts of the castle at Kungelv and see how obviously critical this strategic area had been to Sweden, as it controlled that country's only exit to the western oceans, drove this point home. Thus my personal memories became expanded to include relevant historical descriptions from the era and unfortunately, no doubt, also tainted by personal opinions and interpretations.

I must thank my wife and children for putting up with these stories for over forty years. I am sure that the experiences of my formative years made me encourage an exceptional independence in my children and I am thankful that I never had to send them off alone from a besieged city on their bicycles with nothing but a bottle of milk in the luggage carrier, as my parents had to do when I was nine years old. I also insisted that they know and understand the events of the Second World War, even though to them that war was as remote as the First World War was to me. Thus, "Victory at Sea" reruns were a staple on our first black and white TV.

Finally, I must express my appreciation to my daughter-in-law, Zanne Miller, for her untiring efforts in guiding me in the preparation of this manuscript, while at the same time working and attending to twin daughters.

Peter H. Tveskov
Branford, Connecticut

Chapter 1
Skovshoved

Tuesday April 9, 1940: It was a sunny spring morning after the murk that is the Danish winter. I was five years old and visiting my grandparents in Skovshoved, a suburb about five miles north of Copenhagen. As I slept on a cot at the foot of their double bed, the sound of a swarm of airplanes flying overhead, more planes than I had ever seen before or since, woke me up.

My grandparents on their retirement a couple of years before the occupation began had moved from their villa in the town of Randers, in Jutland, to a four room apartment in Skovshoved. For my cousin Jan (Danish pronunciation: Yæn) and me it was always exciting to visit our grandparents in their new surroundings, although on this occasion I was the only visitor. Jan was my double cousin, two brothers having married two sisters, five months older than I, and the closest to a brother I ever had.

The construction of the new four lane coastal road and new harbor at Skovshoved was just about complete and for five year olds deeply interested in trains and ships, it was an adventure to walk with our grandfather and explore these projects. The new road was edged with a beautiful, broad granite railing and we had a great time walking on top of it. Large boulders from the island of Bornholm were dumped along the curved granite embankment to protect the highway from storms and winter ice. As I grew older we found this a great and convenient place from where to swim in the summer time.

Skovshoved had been a fishing center since the thirteenth century, the fishermen working at first from the beach and later from a small harbor. They would bring their catch to Gammel Strand, the canal next to Christiansborg Castle in the center of Copenhagen, where their women would sell it. One clear memory of those days is the fishmonger selling fresh fish from his pushcart, alerting my grandmother with his call: "Jeg har l-e-e-e-e-vende rødspætter!" (I have l-i-i-i-ve flounders). She would buy fresh flounder, eel, and cod from him, all common parts of our daily diet.

Nowadays the pollution of the Baltic Sea by the former Soviet Union, the German Democratic Republic, Poland, and Sweden has killed much of the fish in the Baltic and all that remains of the *Skovser* women is a statue dedicated to them on Gammel Strand, close to that of the equestrian statue of Bishop Absalon with his battle axe located on Amager Torv (Amager Market Square). It was Absalon who founded Copenhagen about a thousand years ago.

My grandfather Peter Hein, who had retired in 1938 after a career as a successful manufacturer of marine engines, was born in Graasten in northern Slesvig. Since the Danish defeat in 1864 that province had been part of the Kingdom of Prussia until parts of it were reunited with Denmark following a plebiscite in 1920. Although his family was Danish he had been brought up at a time and a place when the Prussian authorities prohibited the speaking, reading or writing of Danish in public. He and his brother, Hans, fled to Denmark in 1899 to avoid service in the Prussian army and had become Danish citizens. He had served his compulsory military service in an artillery unit of the Danish army and had even been recalled during World War I, when Denmark remained neutral. He continued to run his business during that war wearing his blue artilleryman's uniform.

Grandfather was drawn to Skovshoved because of the presence of the commercial fishermen and their wooden boats in the harbor there. He had manufactured and sold two-cycle, single-cylinder semi-diesel engines to them for a generation and there was at least one fisherman—Mr. Sørensen—who had a Hein engine in his boat. My grandfather spent many an hour with fisher Sørensen and the other fishermen in the harbor—even those who had Tuxham, Hundested, and the engines of other competitors in their boats. My cousin and I got to know these men and their boats and could recognize the reversible screw of a Hein engine and the presence of the engine in the boat just by the way its exhaust stack came out through the rounded stern of the boat, not vertically in front of the pilot house as the competitors'.

The new harbor in Skovshoved was built with three basins, one for the commercial fishermen, one for pleasure boats, and one for boat maintenance, complete with a "marine railway." The boats that were to be hauled ashore were placed in a wheeled cradle on railroad tracks, and we would watch it and the boat being pulled up on the dock. The illogic of the railroad tracks disappearing into the water fascinated me. Later on, a breakwater built of more boulders from Bornholm was created in front of the harbor entrance.

A brand new gasoline station was built at the entrance to the harbor. It featured a modern design with a mushroom shaped canopy. The station originally was a Texaco station, but after being closed during the war, it became a Caltex station. The station was designed in 1937 by Arne Jacobsen, a well-known Danish architect, and eventually became a National Landmark.

On occasion, such as in 1942 and 1947, the Øresund would freeze over and so would the harbor. To prevent damage to the wooden piers, the ice would be cut loose creating a large ice floe within the harbor. Permanent boards somewhat like diving boards were installed on the edges of the piers to provide access to the sailboats in the summer. We would climb out on these boards and drop down on the ice, where we would skate. Our skates were strapped to our boots with clamps and tightened by a skate key. The ice from the Baltic's brackish water was knobby and tickled our feet as we skated. To get back up from the ice, we would cross the open strip of water, going hand over hand hanging under the "diving boards" and then climb up on the pier with our heavy skates still clamped to our shoes. One evening I made the mistake of showing my mother how this was done and that was the end of my skating on the harbor ice!

Walking northward along the new highway one came to a break in the railing and stairs leading to the remaining tip of a small peninsula. My cousin and I dubbed it *Den lille ø* (the small island). The new highway ended about two miles further north at

Bellevue Beach in Klampenborg. Inland from the new highway was the Gamle Strandvej (old shore road). The center of Skovshoved was still dominated by the small houses of fishermen and one large building, the Skovshoved Hotel, where itinerant magicians and other performers would perform. There were also the usual small stores and a local movie house, distinguished by a fountain and statue of Venus on a large scallop shell at the center of the stage. The statue—fountain and all—would sink into the floor when the movie was about to begin.

Stretching north and south on either side of the old village on the old shore road stood a number of large villas. Further inland toward Ordrup, there were newer single-family homes and occasional apartment buildings. One of these was "Korsgaarden," a new three-story building where my grandparents had their apartment.

ii ii ii

I was born in October 1934 in Copenhagen and was five years old at the time of the German Occupation. I was 10 when it ended. As anyone who has lived through a war at any age of his or her life knows, those five years undoubtedly shaped me—defined who I am and who I became.

An only child, I lived with my parents in Østerbro, a largely middle-class neighborhood of Copenhagen dominated by large apartment blocks. It was established in the late 1800s as the city's medieval moats and ramparts were abandoned and eliminated, if not turned into parks such as the Tivoli.

My father was born in Randers, the son of a professional warrant officer in the Danish cavalry in the days when the dragoons and hussars still had horses. (I remember visiting my grandfather when he was stationed with the Royal Horse Guard in Copenhagen shortly before his death in 1938. He would take my cousin and me to see the horses in the stables and to this day I remember the almost pleasant smell of that stable.) After serving his compulsory military duty in the Danish Royal Guard in the 1920s, my father became an accountant and worked for the Danish East Asiatic Company (ØK) and was slated to join their operations in Thailand. This did not happen due to his illness, which turned out to be multiple sclerosis. It eventually left him completely paralyzed. His last job was with the weekly magazine *Hjemmet*. He married my mother, his older brother's sister-in-law, in 1933.

Soon after rejoining civilian life he began experiencing the progressive symptoms of MS. Then as now, this disease was not well understood and he underwent many forms of treatment, all unsuccessful. In 1939 he flew to a clinic in Kassel, Germany, for treatment and was there when Denmark was invaded. I remember going to the airport with him to see him off. The plane was a Swedish DC-3 with large Swedish flags painted on it and two Swedish flags flying from the cockpit. It was a foggy morning and the plane eventually disappeared into the mist. Many years later the atmosphere of the whole scene came back to me when I saw the movie Casablanca.

My father returned from Germany and grew progressively worse. In late 1944 he and my mother were granted exit visas by the Germans to travel to neutral Sweden for treatment by a famous Stockholm surgeon, Prof. Olivenkrona. My mother accompanied my father to Sweden, but returned to blacked-out Denmark in early 1945. The visa was arranged through uncle *M*, my father's brother. Part of the arrangement was that I was to stay behind in Denmark as hostage. The swastika stamps in my mother's passport from that trip caused questions and raised the authorities' eyebrows after the war. Thus my father was out of the country at the time of the German invasion and also at the time of the surrender.

My mother, also from Randers, was trained as a gymnastics teacher and taught at a Catholic school there. None of my family was Catholic, in fact my mother was a fairly militant atheist and a "women's libber" before that term existed. When my father had to stop working, she got a job as a telephone operator in the center of Copenhagen in a quasi-official institution, the Industrirådet (The Council of Industries). They divorced in 1947.

When the time came for me to start elementary school in 1941 at Vognmandsmarken School, the neighborhood primary school, it had already been requisitioned and turned into a barracks by the German army. Rather than attending another school in the area, which had been doubled up to accommodate the students from Vognmandsmarken School, it was decided that I should live with my grandparents in Skovshoved and attend school there. Skovshoved, about five miles north of the center of Copenhagen, although still a working fishing village at the time, was emerging as a rather affluent suburban neighborhood with many large villas along and inland from the shore road (Strandvejen) that runs from Copenhagen to Helsingør (Elsinore).

Skovshoved School was and is located one long block from my grandparents' apartment, across the street from Skovshoved parish church. I attended Skovshoved School in grades 1 through 5 from 1941 until entering middle school at Gammel Hellerup Gymnasium in August 1946. Under the educational system in effect in Denmark at the time, everyone had to take a test in the 5th grade at age 10-11, which in effect decided whether you would eventually be able to go to the university. In the 6th grade we started foreign languages, physics, chemistry, and other subjects that in the U.S. would be considered high school subjects. This system was later found to be unfair to slow learners or kids who were poor test takers and has since been changed. However, I did pass the one-day test and was accepted at Gammel Hellerup Gymnasium, a prestigious secondary school founded by the Danish educator Hartvig-Møller. It had only recently become a public school and was then located about three miles south of Skovshoved on Frederikkevej in Hellerup. Depending on the weather, I would either ride my bicycle to school or take the No.14 streetcar down the old shore road and occasionally, during the rare winters when it snowed enough to do so, even ski to school.

My friends and classmates all lived in the neighborhood. My cousin, Jan, lived about a 25-minute bike ride away in Gentofte. The closest railroad station was in Ordrup, about a ten-minute walk from the apartment. We were served by two streetcar lines: the No.14 that ran into Copenhagen along the old shore road and the No.15 from the Ordrup Station to Gentofte and the Center of Copenhagen. To make it easier to identify the streetcar lines, the number signs on them were painted in different color combinations: No.14 had white numbers on a blue-red back ground with the colors separated diagonally; No.15, yellow numbers on a red background; No.6, white numbers on a dark blue background; and No.1, red numbers on a white background. These were the streetcar lines that I would use most frequently and when I started learning numbers in elementary school these color combinations became mnemonic means for me to remember numbers. To this day I still see the numeral six in my mind's eye as white on a blue background.

I respected my grandparents greatly and believed them to have been excellent examples for me. Despite their obvious and demonstrated love for each other, they treated each other with a great deal of respect and formality. As an example, my grandfather always referred to my grandmother as Mrs. Hein. They were married in 1900 when she was 16 and he 24, after the birth of their first daughter, my aunt Didi. In retrospect the arrangement to have me come live with them undoubtedly was an imposition on their retirement, but if they felt it to be so they never made me feel anything but welcome and loved.

I could go to my parents' apartment on Østerbro by either streetcar line and when I stayed at their apartment I would go to school in the morning via the S-Train to Ordrup. However, the bicycle was the most common means of transportation year-round and in all kinds of weather, except snow. Fortunately the Danish weather is known more for its rain than for serious snowfalls. Despite all the insecurities of living in a wartime situation, such as air raid alarms and frequent interruption of service, I often traveled alone to and from Copenhagen by streetcar, train, or bicycle and my grandparents and parents had no compunctions about my traveling alone at such an early age. While we were warned "not to talk to strangers" and to "keep an eye out for weird people," I felt very safe.

My grandfather kept his car in a rented garage a few feet down the road from the apartment. He also had his workshop in the garage, the shop from where produced homemade toys for my cousins and me. The toys consisted mainly of cars, but he also made trains and ships.

What I did not know in 1940 was that till leaving Denmark in 1948, when my mother remarried and we moved to Venezuela, I would spend all of my early years living with my grandparents in Skovshoved. On one hand those were good years, full of happy childhood memories. On the other hand, a feeling of insecurity and impermanence due to the presence of the occupiers was pervasive during the five years of the German occupation, a feeling felt even by the children. We children knew that the only rights and protection we enjoyed were derived from our families and other countrymen, not from the German authorities, who provided neither.

ji ji ji

During a visit to Copenhagen during the summer of 2002 I took an early S-Train to Ordrup Station and walked to my grandparents' old apartment house, from there to the harbor and back to the station by way of my old elementary school. The walk took a lot less time than I remembered, but then my legs were shorter fifty-five years ago. Not much had changed.

Incredibly, the nameplate showing the name of my grandparents' upstairs neighbors in the entryway was the same; I suspect that their daughter lives there now. My grandfather's old garage was still there and at the end of the street, where the Germans had blown up a villa in an act of reprisal, now stood a newer house that seemed to stand out from the rest of its neighbors.

The new shore road had not changed, but only pleasure boats could be seen using the Skovshoved harbor. The tracks of the marine railway had been torn up and a large crane equipped with four large tires was there in its place. One old and rather dilapidated wooden fishing cutter remained in a cradle on the pier, probably as an exhibit. But she had a Hein engine in her!

Arne Jacobsen's 1937 "futuristic" gasoline station was there, but I did not recognize the brand of gasoline sold. The movie house had been turned into a supermarket and the old hotel an apartment house. Many of the original fishermen's cottages were still there, but had been upgraded to quaint-yet-expensive dwellings.

The core buildings of my old elementary school hadn't changed much at all, but new buildings had been added and the soccer field was filled with private homes. There is a plaque in the wall of the church listing about a dozen young men from Skovshoved killed in the war against the Germans. The last entry on the plaque is:

Svend Otto Nielsen, died at age 36, April 27, 1944.

Chapter 2

The Jews

The W family was Jewish and lived across the courtyard of the large apartment building on Østerbro where my parents lived. When the Germans decided to arrest the Danish Jews in October 1943, the W's next-door neighbors hid them at the risk of their lives, while the Germans ransacked their apartment. It must be emphasized that the neighbors who risked their lives were only acquaintances and not personal friends of the Ws.

Denmark was invaded and occupied by Germany on April 9, 1940. The occupation lasted five years, ending when the German forces in Holland, Northern Germany, and Denmark surrendered to British Field Marshal Bernhard Law Montgomery at 6:30 PM on May 4, 1945.

The German occupation of Denmark went through two phases: Following the invasion and occupation, the Danish government engaged in a policy of accommodation. The Danish elected government continued to function, free elections continued to be held, and the Danish Armed Forces were allowed to exist. In contrast with other occupied countries, the relationship between Denmark and the German Third Reich was channeled through the Danish Foreign Ministry, the German Embassy, and the German Foreign Ministry in Berlin—at least in theory.

As Great Britain, Denmark's most important trading partner, was no longer accessible, Danish exports were routed to Germany instead. These exports traditionally consisted primarily of food products such as bacon and butter. Denmark's other major industries—shipbuilding, the manufacture of large diesel engines for ocean going ships, and the manufacture of automatic infantry weapons—were also integrated into the German war effort. Many Danish manufacturing firms obtained subcontracts from German armament and electronics firms. The General Motors assembly plant in Copenhagen manufactured modern Opel "Blitz" trucks for the German army. The economic impact of the invasion and the occupation thus appeared positive on the surface. However, as the purchase of these good and services was financed by the Danish National Bank through loans to Germany, loans to be repaid after the war, this was indeed an illusion.

More than 20,000 Danish workers were recruited to voluntarily work in Germany, replacing German men who were in the army. As there was significant unemployment in Denmark, the Danish government encouraged this recruitment. These workers were not in Germany as slave labor. At least 5,000 Danish volunteers with the blessing of the Danish government joined an SS unit, *Freikorps Dänemark* (Danish free corps), led by Danish officers and non-commissioned officers. A little more than 100 Danish SS veterans today are still collecting their military pensions from the German government.

The German demands on the Danish authorities escalated to the point where they could no longer be accommodated and on August 29, 1943, Denmark's elected parliament and cabinet under Mr. Scavenius resigned. Specifically, the Germans demanded that the death penalty be introduced for acts of sabotage and that the military intervene against work stoppages. The Danish armed forces were promptly demobilized, the navy scuttled, and the officers interned for a while by the Germans. From then until the end of the occupation, the department heads of the various ministries, all career civil servants, carried out the day-to-day administration of the country while the Germans under Dr. Werner Best, an SS general and Reich Plenipotentiary in Denmark, served as the actual rulers of Denmark.

It is important to note that although a Danish Nazi party existed, the *Danmarks Nationalsocialistiske Arbejderparti* (DNSAP), its leadership was so inept that unlike in other occupied countries, the Germans at no time seemed to have seriously considered turning the government of the country over to this party. From the time that the elected Danish government resigned on August 29, 1943, Denmark had been under martial law and the German army of occupation under General von Hanneken had received authority to intervene in the internal affairs of the country. Thus the illusion that Werner Best, the "civilian" plenipotentiary, governed the "Model Protectorate" was just that—an illusion. In reality, General Von Hanneken had supplanted Best thus neutralizing him politically.

ii ii ii

On September 8, 1943, Dr. Best sent an urgent telegram to Foreign Minister Joachim von Ribbentrop, the German foreign minister and Best's superior in Berlin, which became a decisive document in the history of the German occupation of Denmark. In the telegram, Best requested specifically that the *Jüdische Frage* (the Jewish Question) be resolved before martial law in Denmark could be ended. In the telegram he also summarized all the difficulties involved in persecuting the Danish Jews, but it mainly argued for the establishment in Denmark of a government under his leadership, with executive and legislative powers in his name. For this purpose he requested that more German police troops be placed at his disposal. Best was aiming for a political comeback, perhaps as Reich Komisar reporting directly to Hitler. It was important to him not to disturb the status quo in Denmark and not to interfere with Denmark's deliveries of goods and services to Germany. In any event, Best decided to use the Danish Jews as part of his political power play.

Hitler's unexpected reply arrived September 18 in the form of a *Führerbefehl* (Führer's edict) and was thus irreversible: The *Endlösnung* (Final Solution) to the Jewish Problem in Denmark was to be implemented and the Danish Jews deported and eliminated. German police troops subsequently were sent to Denmark in large numbers. Internal power struggles and ill-defined responsibilities were typical in Hitler's inner circle and this strong response to Best's politically motivated plans indicated that there were more players involved in the game in Berlin. (During Best's war crimes trial after the war he insisted that he was expecting a negative answer to the telegram and the

Danish court subsequently acquitted him of planning genocide against the Danish Jews.)

Georg Franz Duckwitz, the Danish-speaking commercial attaché at the German embassy in Copenhagen, who would later become the Federal Republic of Germany's first post-war ambassador to Demark, was assigned to provide shipping to transport the Danish Jews to German concentration camps. Duckwitz was apprehensive and concerned, as he understood that this decision would unleash a strong reaction in Denmark. Best told Duckwitz that the action would take place on October 1 and 2, during Rosh Hashanah, the Jewish New Year.

Duckwitz acted rapidly to find the Jews a safe haven. On September 22 he went to Stockholm to meet with Swedish Prime Minister Per Albin Hansson. Soon after the meeting, the Swedish government protested to Berlin about the order to relocate the Danish Jews. The response to the Swedish protest was strong and clear: Germany would not allow Jewish adults or children to be moved to Sweden to avoid relocation.

However, the German defeats at Stalingrad in December and January 1942-43 and at El Alamein in October 1942, the Allied invasion of Sicily in July 1943, and the arrest of Mussolini had all made strong impressions on both Sweden and Denmark. In Denmark, the setbacks made the August 29, 1943 revolt possible and in Sweden, they encouraged the government to stop allowing the transport of armed German troops to and from Norway and Finland through its territory.

Despite the German refusal, the Swedes now made it clear that the Danish Jews were welcome in Sweden. In Denmark, Duckwitz notified Hans Hedtoft and H.C. Hansen, leaders of the majority Social Democrat party, who in turn warned Supreme Court Attorney C.B. Henriques, the leader of the Jewish Community in Copenhagen. At first, Mr. Henriques refused to believe that persecution of the Danish Jews was imminent, but after this initial hesitation, Duckwitz' warning spread with lightning speed throughout the Jewish community. Nils Svenningsen, the director of the Danish foreign ministry, tried to confront Dr. Best on the matter, but was advised that Dr. Best "was not available."

In 1943 there were 7,800 Jews in Denmark, 2% of a population of 4,000,000. Many belonged to long established families and were influential and respected members of the Danish community; families such as Lachmann, Levysohn, Hertz, Meyer, and Warburg—intellectual pillars of Danish culture and commerce. Others were ordinary people forced to flee as a result of the Russian pogroms before World War I, whose descendents had become members of the Danish community; families such as Besekow, Koppel, and Pundik. Then there were the latest refugees from the Third Reich—poor and not conversant in Danish. A mixed group yet Danes one and all, regarded by their fellow countrymen as neighbors who just happened to belong to a different religion. On these people the Danish people based their moral ultimatum to the Germans.

There was no "Jewish Question" in Denmark. If a question was to come about, it would be a "National Question," for it would be Danes who were persecuted. Werner Best and his German colleagues in Denmark had not planned for this to happen and had in fact inadvertently cooperated by postponing the inevitable *Endlösnung*.

ii ii ii

It may be useful to compare what happened in Denmark to the events in another occupied country: The Netherlands.

Pre-war Netherlands in many ways was like Denmark although it had twice as many inhabitants and 140,000 of them were Jewish. It had, like Denmark, similar democratic traditions and no history of anti-Semitism. When war came, the Dutch queen and government fled to Great Britain and were replaced by Reich Komisar Seyss-Inquart. With him came the slow, systematic, and merciless separation of the Dutch Jews.

One step in that separation was that the Germans now required everyone to carry an *Ausweiss*, a national identification card. On this card each Dutch citizen had to indicate his/her religion, which was predominantly either Dutch Reformed Protestant or Roman Catholic. A Dutchman from that era, interviewed many years ago on a history show on American TV, explained just how insidious the *Ausweiss* was: "As good Europeans we obeyed the authorities and, by identifying ourselves as Christians, by exception immediately identified our Jewish compatriots as such, thus condemning them to death."

Upheavals and strikes occurred among the Dutch in response to the persecutions, but they were suffocated through reprisals against the steadily poorer and terrorized population. This came about as the Germans considered the Netherlands a conquered territory to be exploited. The country therefore never had the relief of a period of accommodation such as Denmark had enjoyed for three years after the German invasion.

The Dutch Jews were placed outside the law, registered, and collected in camps. On June 25, 1943, Jew No. 100,000 was removed from the civic body of the Netherlands. On September 3, 1944, the last transport left for Auschwitz. Anne Frank and her family were on it. Of the 140,000 Jews in the Netherlands, 75% died in the German gas chambers.

ꙮ ꙮ ꙮ

The majority of Danish Jews left their homes when the warning was received. They found refuge with Danish friends and neighbors, or sometimes even with strangers that opened their homes to them. The Germans caught 384 Jews between October 1 and 2, 1943. The rest had gone underground. This created a catastrophic problem. Nearly 7,500 men, women, and children were dispersed, terrified, to unknown addresses, often crowded into one place, making for frighteningly easy targets. Protest rained down on Werner Best from all sides: Churches, labor unions, universities, and of course from the directors of the Danish government ministries.

Sweden now took the final step. On October 2 they released the news of the persecutions in Denmark to the world press, including the news of the rescue action. For the second time since August 29, 1943, Denmark made page one of the world's newspapers.

Thousands of Jews were still in hiding in Denmark. For the Danish population the German action against the Danish Jews was a turning point. No other single event during the war had such an effect: A total mobilization, not only in numbers but also in attitude against the Germans, an attitude similar to that which generally existed in the Allied countries of the rest of the world.

A substructure for the flight to Sweden had to be created. The refugees were shipped to Sweden hidden in boats and ships departing from the east and north coasts of Zealand north of Copenhagen. Most of the refugees had to remain in hiding until an organization was established to handle their transportation. Here the hospitals and physicians of Copenhagen played a decisive role and two thousand refugees passed through Bispebjerg Hospital alone during the first weeks.

Daily meetings were held by a "general staff" at the library of the *Kommunehospital* (Municipal Hospital) in Copenhagen, including the chief of medicine, interns, marine experts, truck drivers, ship captains, fishermen, students, the police, and the Resistance. To locate that many people, move them to other hiding places, and finally transport them to Sweden created obvious financial and logistical problems. Often the attempts had to be aborted and accidents and suicides caused loss of lives. The money came from organizations, businesses, and individuals— including the Jews themselves. The money moved without receipts, delivered to and by unknowns in attaché cases and paper bags, and was hidden in the strangest places. It is remarkable that there is no known case where lack of funding hindered the rescue of a refugee.

Reaching Sweden across the Øresund had been considered nearly impossible prior to this effort due mainly to the strong currents. Some had tried walking across the ice and had perished. Others had disappeared in small boats or had been arrested on the shore. Those who did get across had difficulty with the Swedish police who were alert and officious.

But by October 1943, attitudes were changing and both the Danes and Swedes seemed more willing to take risks to help the Jews. The Danish coastal police, for example, directly assisted the refugees or looked the other way while many Swedes helped the illegal transports once they entered their territorial waters.

A number of German army regulars even proved to be somewhat reticent in their attempts to stop the refugees, and German patrols in Øresund were proved somewhat ineffective in stopping the exodus. And as for Dr.Best, he apparently preferred to see the problem disappear from his political horizon as quickly as possible. On October 2 he telegraphed Berlin: *Dänemark ist judenfrei* (There are no more Jews in Denmark).

The German police, however, were not so accommodating. What it lacked in numbers, methods, ability, and local knowledge, it compensated for with activity and brutality. Poor weather and Danish collaborators helped the Germans somewhat, but overall the results favored the refugees: A total of 7,220 Jews made it to Sweden, 120 perished, some continued to live in Denmark, and 474 went to Theresienstadt, a ghetto prison town in Czechoslovakia between Dresden and Prague. Of those,

58 died, mainly old and sick individuals. There is no recorded case of any Danish Jew dying in one of the German death camps.

The obscene and deadly German racial policy failed miserably in Denmark and led to the end of the effectiveness of the Danish Nazis and their collaborators. It was probably a stroke of luck that events bypassed the civil servants heading the Danish government ministries. Their initial consideration of internment of the Danish Jews would have been as catastrophic as the policy of interning the Danish Communists had been at the beginning of the occupation. The official Danish authorities only lent assistance to those Danish Jews who had been sent to Theresienstadt—and then only after they arrived.

The Germans in Denmark insisted that the problem had been handily put out of the way. However, Werner Best was unable to take advantage of his schizophrenic policy. General von Hanneken remained a formidable rival and soon another was added. Maybe due to his disappointment over the failed action in Denmark, Reichführer SS Heinrich Himmler placed SS General Günther Pancke as Supreme Head of the SS and (German) Police in Denmark, thus creating another rival for Dr. Best.

Three and a half years of the accommodation policy in Denmark had worked well in Germany's "Model Protectorate." The supplies had moved smoothly to Germany and the Danish standard of living was higher than in Germany and way above that of the Dutch. But after August 29, 1943, the Danes knew that they lived in a country at war. Resistance—at least passive—became a popular cause.

That resistance led to the founding of the *Frihedsrådet* (The Freedom Council) on September 16, 1943. Drawing its impetus to organize directly from the action against the Jews, it brought together well-placed groups from Danish society including the Resistance, the hospitals, the police, the military, students, and even some Social Democrats. It was not intended to be an elected government, but rather serve as a gathering of central leadership of many resistance groups with its authority derived solely from the confidence of the people.

Thanks in large part to the refusal by the Danish government and King Christian X to accept even the concept of a "Jewish Question" in Denmark, or to consider it an issue to be discussed with the German occupiers, only a fraction of the Danish Jews perished at the hands of the Nazis (1.6% as compared to 75% of the Dutch Jews, for example). In addition, the Danish authorities consistently refused to identify the Danish Jewish refugees in Sweden as anything but Danish refugees, thus not allowing a wedge to be driven between the Jewish Danes and their compatriots.

While the true story of the Danish Jews is an amazing one in and of itself, the story of how King Christian X insisted on wearing the Star of David if any Dane had to do so is, unfortunately, just a myth. It never became an issue for him, let alone possible, as the Star of David never came to Denmark. The only sample that I ever saw was the one that my friend J's grandmother brought back from Theresienstadt after the German surrender. The family placed it in a place of honor in their living room.

ii ii ii

From the beginning of the war, Sweden had been neutral, leaning toward Germany, her traditional cultural and commercial partner. She had permitted the Germans to ship tens of thousands of troops through Sweden to Norway and Finland. The troops "officially" traveled unarmed in transit to and from leave in sealed trains. However, recently released information shows that the trains were not sealed and that the weapons were carried in the luggage cars. At one point the Germans requested permission for an entire armored division—Division Engelbrecht—to travel from Norway to Finland to fight the Soviets. The Swedish parliament felt that this was too egregious a violation of the country's neutrality and at first refused. It was not until King Gustav V (1858-1950) threatened to abdicate that the government gave in and permitted the transit, thus avoiding a constitutional crisis in the middle of the war.

It should be understood that with notable exceptions, such as foreign minister Christian Günther, the Swedes were not Nazis, but rather traditionally pro-German and that Sweden's remaining historical enemy—once Denmark had been eliminated after the Napoleonic wars—was Russia and its historical successor, the USSR.

As a result of this pro-German neutrality, Sweden was reluctant to admit refugees from Denmark and Norway, especially refugees such as the Jews who would not only upset the Germans, but also create a conflict with Sweden's own

eugenic policies as they related to Jews, Gypsies, Saami, and
other ethnic minorities. After the German defeats in 1942 and
1943, however, Sweden had moved her neutrality in the direction
of the Western Allies and away from the Third Reich.

ii ii ii

The following article appeared in *Politikens Kronik*, October 1,
1988. It was written by Bent Melchior, Chief Rabbi of Denmark,
in connection with the 40th anniversary of the rescue of the
Danish Jews:

"Historical events occur which eventually become dry facts
and a nuisance for future generations of students. Even events
containing a significant amount of drama, as often as not end up
in a category where later generations do not even want to listen
when old people talk about them. Events also happen that by
themselves are not watersheds, but which always will retain their
immediacy. The rescue of the Danish Jews in October 1943
belongs in this category.

"I may not be misunderstood when I say that the event in
itself did not constitute a watershed. But after all, I and those
closest to me were rescued then, so from my private point of view
it was indeed a defining moment! One must point out that in
global terms the number of Jews saved was a very small
proportion of the Jews who fell victim to the Nazi barbarism.
Maybe that was what made it so notable.

"The rescue of those who made it across the Sound to Sweden
was a small light that could be seen from far away in the total
darkness!

"The rescue was irrelevant to the nearly five hundred Danish
Jews who were unable to avoid arrest by the persecutors. It must
be emphasized that this was not due to lack of interest or courage
among the rescuers. In some cases it was just not possible to
cheat the pursuers.

"Certain elements in Danish and Jewish history leave
significant tracks. Although there was no doubt about the
opposition to Nazism and the repugnance that the Danish
population felt toward Hitler's Germany, the persecution of the
Danish Jews opened the eyes of the Danes in a new way to the
evil represented by Nazism.

"Many became involved in the struggle against the occupying power and remained active even when the action was long over. For those of us in flight it was a relief to know that it was impossible for the Germans to trade acceptance of the persecutions by in turn freeing the Danish military officers arrested August 29. This ploy would have worked in a number of other countries - otherwise the argument would not have been tried.

"It was also remarkable that we here saw testimony to the fact that it was possible to integrate a Jewish community into an otherwise Christian population without surrendering Jewish tradition. There is a special reason to emphasize the attitude of the Danish church and its representatives, which to me and many others represent what is best in Christianity. How often have Jews not experienced that church circles have abused Jewish rights by more or less compulsory conversions?

"Cardinal Lustiger in Paris is but one example. In Denmark, Danish Lutheran bishops and priests not only protested through pastoral letters and from the pulpit, but were also active in the rescue work itself. At the same time they did their utmost to insure that those that were persecuted could follow Jewish law in situations where we ourselves would be inclined to dispense with those laws.

"It was unique that October 1943 represented a spontaneous action by a united people, notwithstanding that the presence of a few fools makes complete unity possible! The effort was made by students and professors, physicians, nurses, custodians, greengrocers, shoemakers, taxi drivers and anyone else who came in contact with the rescue effort. We knew the names of some of our rescuers. We know who housed us, but rarely the contact men or fishermen who risked their life and livelihood, or those policemen who showed us the way to the shoreline from where the boats left.

"In 1958 and 1968 we tried to reach out to those anonymous folks who extended the helping hand of friendship. This year we will also meet in Mindelunden [The common gravesite of those executed by the Germans located in Ryvangen where the executions took place] where we will thank those who died, and also those still alive and assure them that our gratitude will never cease.

"We know that most neither wished nor wish to be thanked, which again characterizes the deed. Maybe that is what transforms a friendly gesture in an acute situation into a historic event, when it is not so much a question of gratitude on a personal level, but a situation where humanity and true humanism owe a debt of gratitude to the example of human action here demonstrated.

(Translated by Peter H. Tveskov, 5/23/90, used by permission.)

Chapter 3
The Germans

The history of the duchies of Slesvig-Holsten had always been taught to us as a black and white issue between Denmark and Germany, especially if one's family came from the area. But one of Queen Victoria's prime ministers, Lord Palmerston, once proclaimed that the history of Slesvig-Holsten was so complicated that only three men understood it: Prince Albert, the prince consort, who was dead; a German professor who had gone insane; and he himself—and he had forgotten it.

In 1942, Denmark had already been to war with Prussia and her allies twice within the previous 100 years, in 1848 and 1865. The issue in both wars was the two border duchies, Schleswig and Holstein (*Slesvig* and *Holsten* in Danish).

The reason for the wars had more to do with royal dynastic politics than with nationalism, which still was a new concept in Europe in the nineteenth century. The king of Denmark had been duke of Slesvig and Holsten for centuries and the two territories had lived in reasonable harmony with each other and with the kingdom of Denmark. For centuries large numbers of noblemen from Holsten served at the Danish court and in the Danish government and military. Although privileged nobility as such no longer exists in Denmark, one still finds many German noble family names in Denmark. One eighteenth-century Danish king was quoted as saying that he "spoke French at court, German to his family, and Danish to his dogs."

In ancient times Slesvig-Holsten was inhabited by a number of Germanic tribes, notably the Angles, the Saxons, the Northern Frisians, and various Danish and Scandinavian tribes. The Danish element reached a particularly impressive cultural development in the region. The Danish town of Haithabu near the present town of Slesvig, was a major trading center, as documented by rich archeological finds. The Danes consolidated power in Slesvig by building the *Danevirke,* a fortified defensive barrier across the peninsula. Combined with the river Ejder it kept most invaders, including the Romans, out of Denmark until its final abandonment in the war between Denmark and Prussia in 1864. However, Danish power in Slesvig-Holsten was vulnerable.

The ethnically German area to the south, including Holsten, expanded its economic domain through vigorous trading activity. *Plattdeutsch* (low-German dialect) spread with immigration and Danish-speaking families gradually found it convenient to change languages. *Plattdeutsch* rather than Danish became typical of Holsten and much of southern Slesvig. Even now most inhabitants of the areas both north and south of the current border are naturally tri-lingual in Danish, *Plattdeutsch*, and the Danish dialect *Sønderjysk* (Southern Jutlandish).

In the early 1800s a number of issues surfaced. First, although Slesvig-Holsten always had belonged to Denmark, it was, technically speaking, a separate country. Second, Slesvig-Holsten and Denmark had the same ruler in the person of the Danish king, who was also duke of Slesvig and duke of Holsten. Finally, ancient international treaty obligations between the European royal houses precluded the inclusion of the two duchies into the kingdom of Denmark. This had never become a problem, as it was expected that the same person, the crown prince of Denmark, would always inherit the duchies, thus preserving a Greater Denmark.

However, there was a fly in the dynastic ointment. According to dynastic laws—the so-called salic laws—on which the legal conditions governing Slesvig-Holsten were based, a female could never be ruler. This was not so in the kingdom of Denmark. The king of Denmark at the time had no sons, so it became opportune for the primarily German population of Slesvig-Holsten to observe that by ancient obligations one land—Denmark—should be inherited by the daughter of the king, the crown princess, while Slesvig-Holsten should be inherited by a male, namely Duke Christian Augustus of Augustenborg, a cousin of the Danish king, who was German by speech and custom. Danish interests were simultaneously threatened by Prussia and Austria, the new, powerful, and expansionist German states to the south.

Ethnic Danish citizens of Slesvig-Holsten, the so-called *Ejderdanskere* (Ejder Danes), were panicked by the idea of being separated from their mother country and agitated for the integration of Slesvig-Holsten into the kingdom of Denmark. King Frederik VII of Denmark declared the complete union of Slesvig-Holsten with Denmark in 1848, an act that the Prussian king correctly felt was a violation of the Danish king's feudal oath as duke of Slesvig-Holsten to the king of Prussia. As duke of Slesvig-Holsten—but not as king of Denmark—Frederik VII was by ancient feudal rules a subject of his liege lord, the Holy Roman Emperor. The Holy Roman Empire, as an entity by then, had been succeeded by the German Federation led by the king of Prussia. Encouraged by the anti-German movement in Slesvig Prussia, the Danish king used it as a pretext to attempt to defeat Prussia and seize Slevig-Holsten. Thus, the war of 1848-1850 erupted between Denmark and the German elements in Slesvig-Holsten, supported by Prussia. Prussia's plans, however, were frustrated by the great European powers' concern over the country's new-found aggressiveness and was forced to back down, giving Denmark a strategic advantage followed by the tactical victories in the battles of Isted and Sankelmark.

The treaty of London in 1852 guaranteed the territorial integrity of Denmark and settled the succession in Denmark and Slesvig-Holsten on the Glücksburg branch of the Danish royal house, which derived its claim through the female line. Duke Christian Augustus accepted a financial indemnity and renounced his claim to the two duchies. Denmark in turn guaranteed the inseparability of the duchies, which were to remain *ewige ungeteilt* (forever united).

This was but a strategic retreat for the Germans and later Prussia, led by Bismarck, convinced Austria to take part in the conquest of Slesvig-Holsten in order to liberate their German-speaking population from Danish suppression. Denmark had indeed provided provocation by trying forcibly to eliminate German as an acceptable language in the territory. Austria greedily agreed, the invasion occurred in 1864 and after a series of bloody battles—most famously the siege of Dybbøl—the German allies occupied all of Jutland and Denmark capitulated. Austria got Holsten, Prussia got Slesvig, and the new Danish-German border was moved north to the Kongeå River. However, after the seven week Austro-Prussian war of 1866, Prussia annexed Holsten, creating a unified Schleswig-Holstein.

The Prussians now reversed the Danish policy and began an equally brutal effort to eradicate Danish language and culture in Schleswig-Holstein, prohibiting the use of Danish in any public acts whether civic, educational, or religious. Following the German defeat in World War I a plebiscite was held in Schleswig, which was divided into three zones for the purpose. The northern zone voted overwhelmingly for Denmark, the southern for Germany, and the middle zone voted German with a slim majority, creating a political issue in Denmark that simmered until after World War II.

After the German surrender in 1945, Great Britain offered Denmark the option of unilaterally moving the border south to the Ejder River and thus recovering all of Slesvig. The Danish politicians realized that by 1945 the already German population of southern Slesvig had been augmented by hundreds of thousands of refugees from eastern Germany and that this would create a potentially serious future problem. In a politically brave act the Danish government turned down the British offer, leaving the 1920 border in place.

Thus the *bundesland* (federal state) Schleswig-Holstein was left as a member of the post World War II German Federal Republic, with the Danish minority granted special rights that were reciprocated for the German minority north of the border in what is now known as Sønderjylland (Southern Jutland). It is ironic that the Danish party in *bundesland* Schleswig-Holstein today has achieved significant political power in Federal Germany by controlling the vote of the land by providing a swing vote between the traditional modern German political parties.

ⁿⁿ ⁿⁿ ⁿⁿ

Today, the people in Holsten speak German and those in Slesvig, Danish. While both German and Danish are Germanic languages that share many words, Danish and German differ grammatically and are not mutually understandable. All Danes learn German in school and thus usually speak rudimentary German, although Danes, especially the older generation, prefer to speak English with foreigners, *especially* with Germans.

It is sad to visit parish churches in Sønderjylland and see the tablets listing the young German and Danish men who perished serving in the Kaiser's armies in the First World War. Usually there are two tablets side-by-side, one with Danish names and one with German names. If there is such a thing as decency and respect in warfare, it is demonstrated in the graveyards around Dybbøl in Danish Slesvig, where ferocious battles were fought in both wars. There one will find the graves of groups of unknown soldiers from both sides. Depending on who won the battle and recovered the remains, the gravestones state in either Danish or German respectively: "Her hviler X tapre tyske soldater" or "Hier ruhe X tapfere Dänische soldaten" (Here rest [number of] brave German/Danish soldiers), each gravestone placed over enemy soldiers by the other side.

By 1865, the Prussians/Germans had replaced the English, and especially the Swedes, as Denmark's traditional enemies and there was little question for most Danes as to who the enemy was when the Germans invaded Denmark in 1940. This was especially so in families such as ours, as my maternal grandfather was born and brought up a member of the suppressed Danish minority in Slesvig when it was Prussian.

ji ji ji

The ordinary German soldiers were usually polite, acted correctly, and minded their own business. For them Denmark was a much more pleasant place to serve than on any of the fronts, so they tended to be on their best behavior. The German troops would march through the streets of Copenhagen singing their martial songs such as "Wir Fahren Gegen Engeland" ("We Are Marching Against England"), "Wacht an der Rhein" ("Watch on the Rhine"—the same melody as used in the U.S. song, "Bright College Years"), and the "Horst Wessel" song, celebrating a "martyred" Nazi by the same name.

My father had been hospitalized in Kassel, Germany, at the time of the German invasion. When he came home from the hospital in 1940 he and I, now six years old, would stop by

Vognmandsmarkens Skole, the elementary school that I was to have attended, but which early on had been requisitioned by the German army as a barracks. He would be in his three-wheeled wheelchair and would chat in German with the sentry guarding the entry, using his recently reacquired German to discuss his trip and experiences in Germany. At my age I neither understood nor spoke German, but I remember these encounters as being pleasant and the German soldiers as being friendly. I was also absorbed in the details of their uniforms and weapons. We called them locusts, as they wore gray green uniforms and when going home on leave carried enormous bundles of goods back to the Third Reich. However, it was generally made clear to us children by our elders that, as much as possible, we were to stay away from the German soldiers and ignore them.

ⵊⵊ ⵊⵊ ⵊⵊ

My mother and I went to the small port town of Rødvig, in Southern Zealand, on summer vacation in 1943 and 1944. By 1944 civilians were no longer allowed to go out on the piers. Two middle-aged German soldiers, whom, due to their physical appearance, we referred to as Laurel and Hardy, guarded the piers.

Late one afternoon they saw us walking at the base of one of the piers looking at the vessels in the harbor. My mother was carrying her camera and the guards offered in German and with gestures to take our picture. They took a picture showing us sitting on a bollard out on the prohibited pier in front of a Danish fishing boat.

The two soldiers tried very hard to ingratiate themselves with my mother, who was an attractive woman in her early thirties. They had no success at all, as my mother was not interested and did not speak enough German to be able to carry on any kind of a conversation even had she wanted to. There were quite a few small German vessels in the harbor: Minesweepers, torpedo boats, and many converted small, gray commercial vessels, including a typical Dutch *kogge* with its characteristic leeboards. So while Laurel and Hardy may have felt that they were preventing a Soviet invasion of Rødvig, they soon realized they would have no luck with my mother!

The ordinary Wehrmacht soldiers wore *feltgrau* (gray-green) uniforms. They had little red, white, and black cockades on their caps, some round and some diamond shaped. As they faded, the cockades looked a lot like the British Royal Air Force's red, white, and blue roundel, which could be confusing. Their belt buckles were embossed *Gott mitt uns* (God is with us). The SS wore gray uniforms and had skull and crossbones badges on their hats and SS runes on their collars. The names of their units were printed in gothic letters on a black ribbon on their sleeves, names such as "Totenkopf," "Nordland," and "Leibstandarte Adolf Hitler." I never saw a black SS uniform, but I will never forget the black SS flag flying from Dagmarhus, the building they had confiscated as their headquarters on the City Hall Square. The building still stands and carries the same name.

The German police troops who became more prevalent after August 29, 1943, wore bright green military style uniforms, but without the kepis then worn by the police in Germany. We were aware that they were part of the Gestapo and were intimidated by them, knowing after the first couple of years of the occupation exactly what the SS and the Gestapo were capable of.

As the fortunes of war turned against the Germans, by 1944 the quality, discipline, and appearance of the German soldiers declined. The young men of prime military age had become casualties or had been captured on the battlefields of the Soviet Union, Africa, and Western Europe. They had been replaced with older men, boys from the Hitler Youth, allied troops from Hungary, and even volunteers from Poland and other occupied countries. They were now old men and young boys dressed in bits and pieces of uniforms, both German and Allied. I saw a German soldier on the street wearing an American "Eisenhower jacket" dyed feldgrau, Soviet officer's breeches, and American combat boots. Only his *Scheermütze*—the standard German military "ski cap"—was German army issue. The unit badges, decorations, and other uniform trim became either simplified or disappeared altogether. In many cases metal was replaced with dark plastic.

During most of the war, the German soldier fought in the same uniform that he wore in the garrison, so I suppose some of this simplification was done for camouflage or for economic reasons. For example, the typical German "coal shuttle" helmet, which had taken the place of the *pickelhaube* (traditional Prussian spiked helmet) during World War I, became smaller and less formidable as the war wore on. To save steel, the rolled edges of the helmet eventually were eliminated and replaced with a simple stamped edge. The red, white, and black shields painted on one side of the helmets were eliminated as they were too tempting a sniper target.

In 1945, German hospital trains full of wounded soldiers directly from the front, marked with large red crosses, often pulled into the Østerport station in Copenhagen. We could see the soldiers and their bloody bandages through the windows of our S-Trains as we passed by, a disconcerting sight.

ii ii ii

In 1945, 200,000 German refugees from East Germany and the conquered territories flooded Denmark. They had been told that this was the country that Hitler had promised them and acted accordingly. The refugees walked the streets demanding goods from the Danish stores, refusing to pay for them. We had to get off the sidewalks when we encountered them and walk in the gutter.

They were housed in Danish schools requisitioned for the purpose. We were fortunate that Skovshoved School was not requisitioned, but we did have to share the buildings with another school.

ii ii ii

By the surrender in 1945 a large number of ships of all kinds were anchored off Copenhagen, all filled with refugees. Many would drop their refuse, which included dead bodies and various body parts, directly into the water. Needless to say, that summer swimming was prohibited at Copenhagen's beaches surrounding the now contaminated Øresund.

One day, as I walked along the beach in Skovshoved, I saw a bloated, green German corpse lying on the shore with two Danish policemen standing over it. I did not sleep well for several nights and it was years before the image no longer haunted me.

Chapter 4
The Danes

*One of my elementary school teachers escaped to England
and had returned as a British paratrooper. In the fifth grade he
taught us how to disarm someone pointing a pistol at us.*

Collaborators

Many Danes actively participated in armed resistance against
the Nazis. Still thousands more resisted through non-violent
means. But there were those who chose to collaborate with the
German occupiers, some even taking up arms against their fellow
citizens and donning the invaders' uniforms.

The Danish SS troops, for example, wore gray SS uniforms
with *Freikorps Dänemark* ribbons around the sleeve. On the
completion of their first contract some of these Danish SS men
stayed in Denmark and joined various auxiliary organizations.
Most of the others joined other SS units and many were killed in
battle, including during the final battle for Berlin where SS
volunteer divisions *Nordland* and *Charlemagne* were the last
cohesive German army units left in Berlin.

The first of these Danish auxiliary corps was known as the
Schalburg Corps, named after one of the first commanders of the
Freikorps Dänemark who was killed in action on the Eastern
Front. Christian Frederik von Schalburg was a Danish nobleman.
His mother was Russian and he was born in St.Petersburg. In the

1930s he was a professional officer in the Danish Royal Guard. During the Russian Revolution, the communists murdered his mother's family, so he was fanatically anti-communist. After fighting as a volunteer against the Soviets in Finland, and with the blessing of the Danish government during the period of accommodation, he joined the newly formed Waffen SS unit Freikorps Dänemark. When killed in action, he was buried with full military honors in Denmark.

The original purpose of the Schalburg Korps was to be a Danish Waffen-SS, formed after the death of von Schalburg by Danish Nazis. One of the causes for the general strike of 1944 was that the Germans wanted the Schalburg Korps to wear the uniforms of the demobilized Danish army, a demand that was not met. In 1944 a subgroup was formed under the command of a former Danish officer, Captain Sommer. The purpose of this Sommer Korps was to act as armed watchmen and prevent sabotage.

From the Sommer Korps emerged the Hilfs Polizei (HIPO) whose job it was to counteract the Borger Patrioter (BOPA) and Holger Danske, two Danish, anti-Nazi sabotage groups. But eventually it evolved into a purely terrorist group engaging in "counter sabotage" of trains, civilian buildings, and homes, and committing what it called "clearing murders," reprisal killings of prominent and randomly chosen ordinary Danes.

Another somewhat less disreputable organization of Danish armed and uniformed volunteers in German service were the so-called *Marinevægtere* (Naval Watchmen). Their assignment was the guarding of harbors and shipping.

Friends & the Resistance

Mogens Fog was a well-known neurosurgeon who had my father among his patients. Then, as now, there was no known cure for multiple sclerosis. Surgery was one possibility that was being explored, albeit never successfully executed. My father was hospitalized a number of times in the Military Hospital on Tagensvej under the care of professor Fog.

Fog, who by ideology was a communist, was a leader of the Resistance. He had left the Danish Communist Party no later than the Ribbentrop-Molotov pact between Germany and the Soviet Union (the 1939 non-aggression pact between Hitler and Stalin). He became a leading member of the *Frihedsrådet*

(Freedom Council), the leadership of the Danish Resistance. The Gestapo eventually captured him and he was imprisoned and tortured in the headquarters in the Shell House in Copenhagen. When the RAF bombed the Shell House on March 31, 1945, he escaped and evaded recapture. On the occasion of the German surrender, May 5, 1945, he was named minister for special affairs in the first post-war cabinet. His responsibility was the prosecution of collaborators and the deactivation of the Resistance.

After the Hungarian revolt in 1956 together with Axel Larsen, Fog started a new political party called Venstresocialisterne. Larsen had been the leader of the Danish Communist Party (DKP), and had also been active in the Resistance and a minister in the first post-war cabinet. Fog ended his long and distinguished career as president of the University of Copenhagen. To my knowledge my father never saw him again.

ji ji ji

BA, a successful police detective, was a neighbor and friend of my parents. I remember him as a friendly and happy person with heavy black eyebrows. During the Great Depression he had been apprenticed as a wooden boat builder, but not many wooden pleasure or commercial fishing boats were being built in those days so he ended up as a police officer instead.

Like many police officers he became actively involved with the Resistance. When the Germans arrested the Danish police force on September 19, 1944, he evaded capture and went underground. He moved into my parents' apartment, which was vacant as my father was in a hospital in Sweden, and my mother and I lived at my grandparents' in Skovshoved. My mother told me that to prevent his wife from being harassed by the Germans he officially, albeit temporarily, divorced her. She still lived two entryways down in the same apartment complex. He and JK, a young man who also had gone underground, lived there till the German surrender.

Family & the Resistance

My Uncle O was a Lutheran minister at St. Peter's church in Slagelse, a provincial town on Zealand. Not even my mother's sister, his wife, nor his family knew that he was in the Resistance till he "surfaced" on May 4 armed with an Italian carbine. It had a built-in bayonet that folded back along the barrel. He had deliberately kept even his wife in the dark, so she could not be compromised. After the war he kept the illegal carbine in his office and when I visited him on vacation I would borrow it and play soldier or Resistance fighter in the large garden of the church and parsonage.

Then there was another uncle, OL, who was a gregarious, red-haired high school English and German teacher. OL and my aunt were always the life of the party. He was arrested in the middle of the night at their apartment on Frederiksberg. The reason for the arrest was that my aunt and her sister had lent their summerhouse in Holte outside of Copenhagen to a friend who had gone "underground." He in turn had allowed some young members of the Resistance to hide weapons there including a small artillery piece, and had helped them to do so. The Germans identified the young men. One of them shot it out with the Germans with a machine pistol in the street and was killed. His friend, who was there, was caught and forced to divulge the hiding place of the weapons.

Unfortunately the Germans discovered the friend's identity and picked him and *OL* up on February 24, 1944. My aunt was lucky not to be arrested at the same time, maybe because she was seven months pregnant. The colleagues at her school and other acquaintances were very supportive and she was able to obtain an interview with the Gestapo authorities at the Shell House. They eventually allowed her to bring her husband food and milk at the Vestre prison in Copenhagen. He was released shortly thereafter, but his friend was sent to a concentration camp.

One of my aunt E's university classmates was married to N, a young German who, being opposed to the Nazi regime, had fled to Denmark before the war. Due to the circumstances of his birth—he was illegitimate—there was enough confusion regarding his name, especially since he had a Danish first name that was uncommon in Germany, so that he managed to escape the German draft and ended up studying at the University of Copenhagen. There he met his future wife, a fellow student. They started out helping each other with their respective languages. Eventually the German army found him and he was drafted. He and his Danish girlfriend got married right away before he entered the army. He was fortunate and avoided the most unpleasant assignments of the German army and was used primarily as a courier in Denmark, obviously in German uniform. When with his wife and his mother-in-law, he wore civilian clothes. They moved from an apartment on Maglekildevej behind the French School and by doing so their lives were saved when the RAF accidentally bombed the school. He often traveled in the line of duty on Danish trains and suffered the disparaging remarks from the Danish passengers, who tended to be intimidated by his presence. They were unaware that he spoke Danish and understood everything. After the war he got a good position in Denmark as an archivist in the state archives, where he and my aunt continued to keep in touch.

ϗϗ ϗϗ ϗϗ

My Uncle M, my father's older brother, was a complex character. He, like my father, was drafted into the Royal Guard, but unlike my father accepted the offer to go on to officers' school. He was commissioned and eventually left active duty as a first lieutenant in the reserve. His next step was a life-long career with the Danish State Railroad (DSB), where he rose rapidly as a protégé of Peter Knutzen, the president of the railroad. My uncle successfully headed the public relations branch of the railroad during a time when many service innovations took place, such as the *Lyntog* (lightning trains), new diesel powered fast express trains, the inauguration of the S-Bane, the Copenhagen urban rail system, not to mention the inaugural of the Fugleflugtslinie, the direct rail line between Berlin and Copenhagen via the Gedser-Warnemünde ferry connection.

He worked closely with the German railroads, as by geography and commerce the Danish rail system is thus intimately connected with that of its southern neighbor. It was a fair bet at the time that Uncle M was slated to follow Mr. Knutzen as head of the DSB. This collaboration with the Germans continued during the war, with the blessing and encouragement of the Danish authorities. However, there were indications that Uncle M probably was closer than necessary not only to his German railroad colleagues, but also to other German authorities in Denmark. He was the Secretary of the Danish-German Association of which Mr. Knutzen was president.

He traveled to Germany a number of times during the war and received a German decoration on one of these trips. On at least one occasion, he and Mr. Knutzen attended a social affair where Hitler was present and spoke. When tried for collaboration after the war, he was accused of entertaining German officers in uniform in his home, which was felt to have gone beyond the absolute minimum social requirements of his job.

Within the family it was very clear, even to someone as young as I was, that when Uncle M was in the room, the conversation became very neutral and no subject was broached that referred to friends in the Resistance or events involving politics. This situation was awkward and became more strained as the years went by. On the day after the German surrender, he appeared very briefly wearing a Resistance armband, but was soon arrested, tried by a Civil Service court, and demoted. He was further humiliated by being "drummed out" of the Royal Guard. His demotion within the civil service was eventually reversed, but his army commission was never reinstated. He gave his uniforms, dress sword, and other accoutrements to my cousin and me to play with. He continued working for the railroad until he retired, but also became a very successful writer of a series of children's books after the war.

To this day I really do not believe that Uncle M was a Nazi. He probably was an ambitious opportunist who bet on the wrong horse.

ii ii ii

My aunt A was a judge in Copenhagen. She limped as a result of having had polio as a young woman, but had the distinction of being one of the few Danish women who became admitted to the bar in the early part of twentieth century. After the war she received an American University Women scholarship and attended the Yale Law School, where she earned a JD. When she retired from the court, she was knighted with the Order of Dannebrog. In her retirement and shortly before her death, her little house in Glostrup outside of Copenhagen was broken into and the medal stolen. Glostrup used to be a desirable middle class suburb west of Copenhagen, but has since become crime ridden and heavily populated with Muslim "asylum seekers." Her sister recently sent me a letter from the headquarters staff of the Danish Navy written to her in July 1945. In the letter, the navy expressed its appreciation for my aunt having provided it with a place to meet after the navy had to go underground following its demobilization from August 29, 1943, until the German surrender in 1945. Until receiving that letter I was not aware that she had been involved with the Resistance in any way.

ii ii ii

My grandfather thoroughly disliked and mistrusted Germans and anything German. Although probably one of the most law-abiding, kind, and generous persons I have ever known, he had a serious aversion to any kind of police due to his childhood relationship with the Prussian gendarmerie. Right after the war, while driving in his car with a friend of the family and me, a kid shattered the windshield of the car with a slingshot. We went to the boy's home where my grandfather made what he thought were appropriate arrangements with the boy's father. However, the family friend meanwhile had called the police to have a report written for insurance purposes. When the police officer arrived on his bicycle, my grandfather became as upset as I had ever seen him. It was difficult for the family to accept that my grandfather reacted to the rather benign Danish police officer on his bicycle as he would have to a Prussian gendarme! Although kind and helpful in all other ways, when we started studying German in the seventh grade, he absolutely refused to help me with my homework.

During the last year of the war he carried a syringe with alcohol in his pocket to be used as a weapon against the Germans, should they try to arrest him or draft him into the German army, a draft he had avoided forty years earlier. He told me that he intended to spray the alcohol in the eyes of any German who tried to catch him. While speaking and writing perfect Danish, my grandfather had a German accent till the day he died.

ii ii ii

While I lived at my grandparents' in Skovshoved and went to school there, I did on occasion go alone or with my mother to my parents' apartment on Østerbro to pick up things. On those visits I was intrigued by the guns and ammunition stashed there. Loaded magazines for British Sten guns and Swedish *Husquarna* machine pistols were stashed under my parents' bed. Even the spinet piano was filled with ammunition boxes!

On May 5, after having been celebrating the Liberation in the center of Copenhagen, my mother and I went to the apartment and while I watched, she took a box of cartridges for the standard Danish army *Kragh-Jørgensen* rifle from the piano as a souvenir. She put it back in the piano once BA and JK had moved out of the apartment. It must have come as quite a surprise to the piano tuner when the piano was tuned for the first time after the war!

Chapter 5
Daily Life: Shelter, Food, Clothing & Money

Silk and later nylon stockings of course were the gold standard and could be exchanged for just about anything during the war if one could find them. Some Danish women would paint a "seam" up the back of their tanned legs with make-up to appear to be wearing silk stockings.

Shelter

A housing shortage developed during the Occupation as resources were increasingly diverted to the German war effort. Thus, housing was carefully rationed and it was difficult to rent or purchase an apartment, especially if one already had some place to live. This bureaucratic nightmare continued till long after the War and its remnants still exist even today. It could create awkward situations. When my parents were divorced my mother moved into an apartment next door to the co-op apartment she had shared with my father. My father's widowed mother had lived in that apartment and now moved in with my father. To avoid contact, my father and grandmother used the street side entrance to the building, my mother the courtyard entrance.

To assuage the housing shortage during the war, an old section of the inner city of Copenhagen was "sanitized," as it was called in those days. Half-timbered slum tenements dating back to the Middle Ages were torn down and new apartment blocks built.

However, regulations were passed that due to the shortage of coal, new apartment buildings could not have central heating systems. Individual wood or coal-burning stoves were installed in each apartment and the tenants had to fend for themselves. The concept of Danish Design was already in place and these stoves were actually quite attractive. But after looking at one of the new apartments, my mother decided that she would rather live next door to her ex-husband than have to feed a wood-burning stove!

In apartment houses, heat and electricity were also rationed. That meant we could heat only one room of the apartment at a time. Fortunately, the Danish climate is wet but rather temperate, and so this was usually not a major hardship. We would bring our feather bed comforters into the heated room before going to bed and warm them on the radiators.

ii ii ii

Elaborate fortifications were built along the western coast of Jutland as part of Hitler's Atlantic Wall. These fortifications were designed by the Germans, built by Danish contractors, and paid for by the Danish national treasury, which also footed the bill for the upkeep of the German occupation troops. Because the invasion never came, the fortifications were never tested. The sand dunes soon shifted, and some of the bunkers rolled down to the beach like giant building blocks where they still lie today, some of them now out in the water as the shoreline moves to and fro. People sunbathe in their lee and children play in and on them. The Danish contractors must have taken pride in their work because today, 50 years later, the concrete building blocks may be broken but the concrete itself has not deteriorated.

Extensive fields of land mines protected the fortifications. Uniformed German soldiers under Danish command were kept in the country for four or five years after the German surrender to remove the mines, but no attempts were ever made to remove the bunkers, a futile task in any event. Nature has to take its course.

Another mammoth defense project was to build underground, igloo-like air raid shelters with square ventilation turrets on the surface. The space in front of the City Hall had been built as a giant recessed scallop and was aptly known as *Muslingeskallen* (The Scallop). The Germans demolished it and installed the shelters in its place. They also built the shelters elsewhere in the city. After the war the turrets of the shelters were knocked off and the square leveled. For us kids it was exciting to sneak into these bunkers and play war. The signs told us not to, but they could not be locked as they had to be accessible in case of an air raid. Walking through the city today one still comes across groups of these shelters, now overgrown with shrubs and trees. Some were maintained during the Cold War, as they supposedly would resist anything but a direct nuclear hit.

Food

As Denmark was a food producing country that exported agricultural products mainly to Great Britain before the war, food never really became a problem. The surplus food production was exported to Germany instead of England in exchange for coal, fuel, and some manufactured products. Food was rationed and while the selection was limited and the rations decreased as the war wore on, no Dane starved during the war. Toward the very end the weekly individual butter ration was down to about the size of the butter patty we today are used to getting in a restaurant. People then, as now, used a lot of lard on the brown pumpernickel of the traditional Danish open sandwiches. Foodstuffs that were imported or depended on imported components for their production disappeared. Thus, there was little or no coffee or tea available, let alone margarine, chocolate, or tropical fruits.

While beef was rationed, the supply of beef actually remained static or increased. This due to the fact that the Danish soil had been worn out and agriculture depended heavily on imported artificial fertilizer and cattle feed, both of which were no longer available. The farmers therefore had begun to reduce their herds, an untenable position as it eventually would result in no beef at all and worst of all, no dairy products. We also ate some horsemeat, which I remember as it was not part of our regular diet.

Fortunately, the war ended before the situation became acute. If a housewife had a good relationship with the local butcher, beef was available. Fish was plentiful in those days and then as now was a staple of the Danish diet. Unfortunately, the pollution of the Baltic by the USSR, Poland, and Sweden, and over-fishing in the North Sea, today has made fish much rarer and expensive, especially cod and herring.

Attempts were made to produce wine and tobacco in Denmark, but the climate does not lend itself to those crops. I am told that both were awful. Ersatz coffee was also produced, but I never heard anyone praise those efforts. Of course, as in all wars, nearly anything could be bought on the black market at a price. People who had contacts with the Allies, Swedes, or the Germans were usually able to obtain limited amounts of these products without using the black market. And city dwellers who had the opportunity to visit a farm, would revel in "normal" rations of butter and milk—milk that would actually leave a white coating inside the empty glass (the bottled milk in the cities left no more of a coating than water would have done).

The German soldiers had their own trading system, exchanging consumer products obtained from the occupied countries. Denmark, for some reason, was a favorite source of shaving soap for the German soldiers. I suppose it was a product that could easily be transported, traded, and would not deteriorate.

The British would include cigarettes and coffee in the containers with arms and explosives that were parachuted to the Resistance. Stories were told of people finding themselves in awkward situations when stopped by the Germans with a pack of *Players' Navy Cut* cigarettes in their pocket. This was no idle problem as the Germans would conduct so-called *razzias* where at random all traffic on a street was stopped (in those days mainly pedestrians, bicyclists, and streetcar passengers) and they demanded to see everyone's "papers." Every adult had to have a national picture ID card, the so-called *Ausweiss*. The words "Ausweiss bitte," barked by a German soldier, were probably the most feared German words that most Danes sooner or later would hear. If they did not have their ID card they would be arrested on the spot, hauled away, and held at the discretion of the Germans. The children were given cloth ID cards with their names and addresses, very much like Catholic scapulars, to be worn around their necks. We always lost them and I do not remember ever wearing mine.

People collected their cigarette butts and kept them in little bakelite cases, rolling new cigarettes from the leftover tobacco. I once saw a man jump from the platform to the track in the main railroad station just to collect a few cigarette butts from between the tracks. Cigarette paper had to be purchased on the black market, but my grandfather found a cheaper source—psalm book or Bible paper, which he could buy at the stationery store. He had a little gadget with which he rolled cigarettes using pipe tobacco and second hand tobacco from butts. Many an evening I was delegated to making cigarettes, as we all sat together in the one heated room of the apartment talking, reading, and listening to the radio or playing cards. Cigarettes also became a form of currency that non-smokers could use to trade with friends for other scarce products.

My grandmother had a childhood friend who lived in East Orange, New Jersey. As soon as the war was over, he and his wife started sending us gift packages of food and other things that we had not seen in years. Once he had heard somewhere that there was a shortage of salt in Europe, so he sent her a package with salt. The thought was most certainly appreciated, although there really was no salt shortage. Another time he sent my grandmother a package full of beautiful, dark green wool knitting yarn, which was also much appreciated. He had stuck a few Hershey bars inside the package. The yarn was protected with mothballs and the naphthalene smell had penetrated the chocolate bars, but we ate them with gusto anyway. I also remember one of the first days after the German surrender, a shipment of bananas arrived in Copenhagen. Each child was allowed one banana, my first since 1940. My friend J who had just returned from Sweden where bananas were not a rarity, gave me his, so I got two. That was a great day.

I believe that our simple diet resulted in a generation of Danes with good teeth as much as did the dreaded bi-annual free visits and treatments by the school dentist—a feature of the Danish system of socialized medicine!. Extractions without anesthesia were common—after all they were mostly baby teeth—and nobody had ever heard of anesthesia for routine drilling and filling of cavities. I guess that those dentists had not been taught that baby teeth have roots until ready to fall out on their own.

Clothing

Like nearly everything else, clothing, especially adult clothing, was strictly rationed. Everyone wore recycled, patched, and altered clothes of one sort or another and it was fortuitous that both my mother and grandmother were competent seamstresses. My grandmother would knit wool underwear for the kids in the family—oh how it itched! Knitted clothing that had reached the end of its useful life was unraveled and the yarn used again. Synthetic cloth and thread based on cellulose was available. Cellulose, being closely related to paper, however, did not fare well in Denmark's damp climate.

Stockings and socks were patched with patches on top of patches. Darning socks was one of the important skills we learned as Boy Scouts, besides learning to be Resistance fighters in the woods. When I first came to the U.S. in 1949 and showed my aunt in Hackensack my "darning egg" complete with yarn and needles, she contemptuously told me: "In this country we buy new socks, we do not darn them." I have not darned a sock since.

My grandmother made me a Boy Scout shirt out of gray material, but was unsuccessful in dyeing it the appropriate khaki color. So I wore a dark brown Boy Scout shirt for a while until new shirts came on the market. The reverse was true for a troop of Boy Scouts from the Danish minority in Schleswig-Holstein in Germany, who attended the Scout Jamboree in Copenhagen in 1947. They had dyed their former Hitler Jugend shirts a patchy royal blue.

Right after the surrender, British battle dress with its short jackets and multi-pocketed pants became popular among the young people. Using the material from one of my grandfather's suits, my grandmother made such an outfit for me. She was not sure of the details of the belt at the rear of the jacket, so one day on a crowded train she sneaked up behind an English soldier and without his noticing it folded up his jacket to get her answer. A year or so later the British, true to their tradition as traders, placed actual surplus British army battle dresses on the Danish market, dyed a dark navy blue. I had by then outgrown my homemade outfit and was thrilled to be given a real battle dress—even if it was blue rather than olive drab. Ten years after the war, surplus U.S. Army trench coats were marketed in Denmark labeled with the name of a well-known Copenhagen department store. My sweet grandmother bought me one of these trench coats and sent it to me in New Haven, Connecticut, where I was studying at the time.

The bottom line of course is that we really looked pretty threadbare all around. As we did not have much hot water, we probably did not smell too good either, but when everyone is in that condition I guess nobody notices.

Money

Before the war Denmark minted its smaller denomination coins in copper. These copper *øre* coins, which represented 1/100 Krone, came in denominations of one (the size of a U.S. penny), two (the size of a quarter), and five *øre* (resembling a 50-cent piece). There were also 10 and 25 *øre* coins, but they were made of a copper/nickel alloy and silver colored. What all these coins had in common was a hole in the middle, put there to help blind people recognize the various coins and distinguish them from the one and two Krone coins, which did not have holes in them. (*Øre*, the name of the Danish cent, comes from the Latin *aurum*, meaning "gold.")

To put things in perspective, the Danish Krone was worth about one English shilling, then as today about 15 U.S. cents. Of course, 15 cents in 1939 was a whole lot more than 15 cents today. Inflation had caused the value of the *øre* as expressed in any kind of gold value to be miniscule, but at some point in the dim dark past, there really was a gold value to that coin.

Chapter 6

King Christian X
& the Resistance

The degree of resistance must be looked at in the same manner as the degree of collaboration. In order to live and survive, every member of Danish society collaborated one way or another, from the king who telegraphed Adolf Hitler, to the streetcar driver who hauled German soldiers on his crowded streetcar. But what must not be forgotten is that an armed partisan not wearing a uniform or military insignia could legally be summarily executed under the Geneva Convention. Thus it was no trivial matter to join the Resistance, even at the very end of the Occupation.

Before beginning a discussion about the Resistance, it must be understood that under the Geneva Convention and the accepted rules of warfare, a "belligerent who engages in armed warfare, not wearing a uniform or signs of rank, can be considered an irregular and is not covered by the protections offered soldiers by the Geneva Convention." Traditionally all sides under the accepted rules of the Geneva Convention have summarily executed such irregular belligerents. This is significant, as it puts into perspective the risks taken by all members of the Danish

Resistance, whether they joined the effort on the first day of the Occupation or on the last.

It is especially important to understand that unless members of the Resistance were lucky enough to be caught by the Danish police, tried under Danish laws, and imprisoned in Danish jails, they would be subject to investigation and torture by the Germans and their Danish auxiliaries. That, until granted the relief of execution in Ryvangen. Thus, active resistance to the German occupiers was no trivial matter.

King Christian X

I saw King Christian X a number of times. On his 70th birthday in 1940, I watched as he drove through the streets of the city in his Cadillac touring car receiving the people's tribute. My cousin and I stood on a balcony of the Palace Hotel on City Hall Square with our grandparents and took in the spectacle.

Five years later on May 5, 1945, the king and queen rode across the City Hall Square in the same open Cadillac celebrating the Liberation. This time I was on the other side of the square standing on the roof of the office building where my mother worked. From there we had a first row balcony view of all the activities and parades related to the Liberation. The old king by now looked frail and was very ill. Following an accident with his horse he eventually had a gangrenous leg removed. He only lived two more years.

On the king's birthday—a National holiday, thus no school—it was traditional for us kids to go to Amalienborg, the Royal Palace, to see the Royal Guard parade in its red dress uniforms and to greet the king and his family as they waved to us from the balcony. King Christian X in many ways symbolized the sentiments and actions of the Danish people. As a constitutional monarch without any legal authority, he managed to be a true national leader and an example to the Danish people.

Denmark had been a constitutional monarchy since 1849, when the last absolute king granted his people a Constitution; a concept very hard—especially for Americans—to understand today. It took at least a hundred years for the traditions of the royal family to really catch up with the concept that their royal status came from the Danes, and that the Danes were not their "subjects." Not that Denmark was not blessed with reasonably good kings in the formative years of the Danish democracy, but the game was still a ballet of dynastic politics among the royalty of Europe, all of whom were closely related. Between Queen Victoria of Great Britain and King Christian IX of Denmark a large number of reigning kings and queen consorts were created. King Christian IX was known as Europe's "Father-in-Law," one daughter being queen of England, another czarina of Russia, and a son who was king of Greece, just for starters.

Every year these royals would visit one another's countries on state visits. They would throw parties and give each other high decorations, dividing their time between their ocean going yachts and palaces. The common people were given the day off and would bow and curtsy in the streets, doffing their hats as the high personages paraded past. Traditionally the visiting monarch would wear a general's uniform of the host country's army. The fact that these "generals" periodically would have their armies face each other in bloody battles did not seem to affect them one way or the other.

The language at the Danish court prior to the twentieth century was as likely to be German as Danish, as much of the Danish royalty came from the border lands between Denmark and Prussia. Christian X was Danish born, albeit married to a German princess, Alexandrine of Mecklenburg-Schwerin. Queen Alexandrine took her role as Queen of Denmark very seriously, even when Denmark was invaded by her former fatherland. She learned and spoke Danish perfectly, a difficult thing for a German to do, no matter how well intentioned, but nonetheless expected of a nineteenth century princess from any country.

King Christian's brother, Carl, was elected king of Norway as Hakon VII by the people of Norway when that country declared her independence from Sweden in the early part of twentieth century. Although a popular monarch, he never did master Norwegian perfectly. Christian's oldest son, Crown Prince Frederik, married beautiful Princess Ingrid, daughter of the heir to the Swedish throne, and eventually became King Frederik IX of Denmark, father of the current Queen Margrethe II.

So Christian X came from a tradition in which royalty in Europe was still important politically and the emerging constitutional monarchies in Great Britain and Scandinavia were still the exception rather than the rule. Christian X became king on the death of his father, Frederik VIII, a frequent companion of his infamous brother-in-law, the playboy future Edward VII, eldest son of Queen Victoria, who was Prince of Wales for 60 years. Frederik VIII disappeared one evening during a "private" visit to Hamburg and after a frantic search his body was found the next day in a public morgue in the infamous *Reperbahn,* or red light district.

Christian X became king in 1912, at the age of 42, during a time when tremendous change had come to the Danish body politic. The political pendulum had swung from the dominant agrarian and bourgeois parties to the Social Democrats, who represented the emerging class of industrial workers. The Social Democrats were very much a revolutionary party, complete with red banners and all the trappings.

There are indications that Christian X had some problems with the Social Democrats and their revolutionary ideas at the beginning of his reign, problems that did not seem to harmonize with the still developing Danish democratic process. There are recorded incidents when the king might possibly have overstepped his bounds in the constitutional process of selecting a cabinet. Fortunately the relationship between the king and Thorvald Stauning, the leader of the Social Democrat party and the king's prime minister for most of the first half of the twentieth century, matured to one of mutual cooperation and a respect for the new constitutional, democratic tradition of the country. Mr. Stauning by trade was a cigar maker, and he and the still aristocratic king were able to complement each other and work for the good of the Danish people.

After the German occupation, the king as head of state had to continue to carry out his constitutional and ceremonial duties. Acting in full consultation with Prime Minister Stauning's constitutional government, he, as commander in chief of the armed forces, ordered them to cease the futile armed resistance to the invaders. As Denmark theoretically still was an independent nation and all dealings with Germany went through the embassies and the respective foreign ministries, he also had certain ceremonial obligations vis-a-vis Germany, which he kept to an absolute minimum. For instance, he did not receive Dr. Werner Best, the German Plenipotentiary, claiming a diplomatic illness, but shunted him off to his son, the crown prince. And when diplomatic etiquette once required him to attend a German parade, he sent his younger brother, Prince Harald, who "reviewed" the parade from inside his closed limousine.

Hitler was exceedingly upset when the king responded to the official congratulatory telegram for his 70th birthday with a curt,

"Danke, Christian Rex." The joke at the time was that Hitler had suggested that the time had come to unite the two countries, and that the king had politely responded that he was too old to rule over such a large country.

Probably the most significant, symbolic, and important act of leadership that King Christian X carried out was to continue his daily morning horseback rides through the streets of Copenhagen. He would leave the royal palace on his horse, wearing his general's uniform, and ride through the streets alone, surrounded only by the people on their way to work. Two priceless photographs exist from those days: One shows the king on his horse in a crowd of people on bicycles waiting for a traffic light to turn green. The other shows two German soldiers stiffly saluting the king, who totally ignores their salute. The statue erected to the memory of Christian X in Copenhagen shows him on his horse, larger than life. He was.

This king knew his job. Through his own behavior and with only moral authority he became a true leader of all loyal Danes, a man respected by all. Few countries were as lucky as Denmark to have had that kind of leader. On the occasion of Christian X's 70th birthday a small badge was created to be worn as a lapel pin by men and women. It was a small, rectangular Danish flag surmounted with the royal crown and with the initials *C-X* in the middle. The badge was known as *Kongemærket* (The King's Badge) and it was sold in steel, silver, or gold. The proceeds of the sale of these badges went to the survivors of those who had fallen on April 9, 1940. Innumerable people throughout the Occupation proudly wore this little badge, probably not as much as a sign of defiance against the Germans than as a sign of support for Denmark. My younger son still has mine.

The Resistance

When Germany first invaded Denmark in 1940, while not liking it, the majority of the Danish people essentially decided to sit it out. This was to be the third war with Germany in a century and so was largely thought of as yet another altercation between European states. Denmark, because of its strategic location as the "cork" in the Baltic Sea, would survive it one way or the other, as it always had in the past. Since the end of Denmark's role as a major European power following the Napoleonic wars, her position had been protected by the remaining great powers, none of which wanted any of the others to control access to the

Baltic. While there was little public sympathy for Germany, and none for the National Socialist ideology, there was also little overt or covert resistance.

Eventually, however the German occupation became one of true military occupation and Denmark became an official police state with all that implies. Many of those who had earlier adopted a "sit it out" policy now changed their opinions and became active in the Resistance. Following August 29, 1943, the lines hardened and with the active cooperation of the Danish police, the Danish Resistance engaged in significant acts of sabotage against manufacturing plants that worked for the German war effort and against the main railroad lines in order to disrupt the transport of war materiel to Germany and troops to Norway.

The first Danish sabotage group was organized by high school students in Aalborg in Northern Jutland. They called themselves the Churchill Group and when arrested by the Danish police, regularly escaped from the Danish prison at night to carry out their dangerous harassment of the Germans. Later in the war, three principal sabotage groups dominated this activity: Borgerpatrioter (BOPA), originally a Communist group; Ringen, or "the ring" in English; and Holger Danske—named after a mythic giant of the same name who slept under Kronborg Castle in Elsinore, only to awaken when the country was in peril. There were many other resistance groups with different specialties: Intelligence gathering, counterfeiting of documents, smuggling of refugees out of the country, and publishing of illegal newspapers.

The Germans and their Danish auxiliaries, The Schalburg, Sommer, and Hilfspolizei (HIPO) corps, responded brutally to these "saboteurs." The HIPO worked for the *Geheime Staatspolizei* (German Secret Police), better known as the Gestapo. They wore black uniforms, usually with riding breeches and laced-up high boots. From observing and learning of the activities of these criminals and in some cases actually being acquainted with members of the HIPO corps, Danes feared and hated them more than the Germans for their treason and unchecked brutality. For every German train sabotaged, a Danish passenger train was often blown up and Danish hostages were carried in the German military trains. For every factory hit, a Danish newspaper, cultural club, restaurant, place of entertainment, or private home was destroyed.

Individual German soldiers were rarely targeted by the Resistance. Such actions were considered counterproductive and on the rare occasion when individual German soldiers were killed, the reprisals against the civilian population were harsh. Resistance members and civilians were killed and high fines assessed against the municipality in which the killing had taken place. This does not mean that German soldiers and members of the Resistance alike did not perish during sabotage actions.

The Resistance, particularly the members who were Danish police, collected information on traitors and collaborators for use after the war. They also hijacked or destroyed the registers of the Danish churches, which kept most civil records, and produced illegal identification documents as needed.

The Danish police attempted to intervene in cases of sabotage. When the Danish authorities caught the saboteurs, they would be tried before Danish courts and imprisoned in Danish jails. If caught by the Germans the best they could hope for, following interrogation and torture, was to be sent to German concentration camps, principally Buchenwald and Neuengamme. Many were court martialed, executed, and buried in Ryvangen, not far from my parents' home.

On September 19, 1944, the Germans, in an attempt to eliminate any cooperation between the Danish police and the Resistance, issued a false air raid alarm. Because the Danish police officers were required to report to their stations during an air raid, the Germans knew their trap couldn't fail. When the officers arrived they were arrested en masse and immediately shipped to concentration camps, where many succumbed due to forced labor and harsh treatment.

In addition to those directly involved with the Resistance, the general public did what they could to make it clear to the German invaders that Denmark, while occupied, was not yet defeated. In line with the patriotic sentiment of the *Kongemærke*, Danes would gather in the thousands on the *Fælledparken* (Copenhagen Commons), the large park outside the old walls and moats of the city. The huge crowd would picnic on the grass and sing patriotic Danish songs during the long spring and summer evenings, often led by well-known singers from the Danish theatre. The festive feeling of these demonstrations of patriotism and fellowship, even for those of us of a tender age at the time, will never fade.

Another sign of protest was the wearing of the so-called *RAF hats*. They were small, knitted beanies, somewhat like Jewish yarmulkes, in the red, white, and blue colors of the roundels on the British Royal Air Force planes. They became so popular that by 1943 the Germans outlawed them. It was a huge moral victory for the Danes and their traditional subtle sense of humor. My younger son also has my RAF hat.

As the years went by and the German tyranny increased, things gradually changed and more and more people began actively opposing the occupiers. In response, the oppression escalated.

One such escalation included the imposition of the death penalty for acts of sabotage—an act that in many ways led to the resignation of the Danish government on August 29, 1943. The Germans also wanted Danish saboteurs to be imprisoned in German jails and concentration camps. At first they promised that Danish prisoners would go no further south than the Frøslev Concentration Camp right on the German border. The Frøslev camp was unique, in that it was built in Denmark by the Danish authorities and actually operated by the Danish penal system, albeit guarded by German soldiers. The Germans eventually reneged on this agreement and Frøslev became merely a transit point to camps in Germany. Altogether, about 1,000 Danes died in captivity in Germany.

ii ii ii

The Allies and the Danish Resistance collaborated as much as possible. Allied planes would parachute in containers with weapons, ammunition, radio equipment, and explosives. Certain resistance groups specialized in receiving and distributing these materials. This was very dangerous work, as the Germans would attempt to locate the reception points and intercept the deliveries.

Some of the weapons supplied by the Allies included British *Sten* submachine guns, Swedish *Husquarna* machine pistols, U.S. M-1 carbines, Danish *Kragh Jørgensen* army rifles, and a variety of handguns. Explosives were usually of the plastic variety. As my parents' apartment in their absence was used by a couple of members of the Resistance, I became quite familiar with these weapons, which were stored there.

The Resistance also had another type of weapon in its arsenal. As all Danish newspapers were severely censored, one of the most useful and effective efforts was its publishing of underground newspapers, usually mimeographed in basement print shops (one of these print shops was located in the basement of a Copenhagen hotel requisitioned by the occupiers for officers on leave). Trusted intermediaries and then "newsboys" distributed the papers. Even I on occasion carried some in my school backpack to trusted neighbors, probably my only direct contribution to the war effort!

The only sources of news other than the underground papers were the BBC broadcasts in Danish from London and Swedish radio. The Germans jammed the BBC and so to circumvent that problem people made small antennas shaped in the form of crosses. These antennas were illegal and one could be severely punished if found with one, or for listening to London or Sweden at all for that matter. The Germans on occasion patrolled the streets in vans with range finder antennas on the roofs of their vehicles. We thought they could spot our small illegal antennas, but realistically speaking, they were probably looking for transmitters, not receivers. Every evening we gathered around the radio and listened with our ears glued to news from the outside world. One positive side effect was that we all learned to understand Swedish quite well.

ⵊⵊ ⵊⵊ ⵊⵊ

Who was in the Resistance? We all directly or indirectly knew people who were members. One thing is for sure, those who were, did not talk about it much, then or now. I am suspicious when I hear people today describe their adventures in the Danish underground to groups of admirers. Quite a number of people appeared in the days after the Liberation wearing the Resistance armband—a wide blue band with two narrow red stripes, one narrow white stripe, and a little metal disk embossed with the Danish national coat of arms sewn in the middle. It's not that I doubt some of these people were members of legitimate resistance groups, but the question is how many had been so from the early days when resistance was not the popular thing to do and even the Danish authorities discouraged it?

Either way, the important thing to remember is that a great many ordinary people did very extraordinary and brave things—such as the next-door neighbors who hid our Jewish friends while the Germans, within earshot, ransacked their apartment. Or Svend Otto Nielsen, nom-de-guerre "John," a school teacher in Skovshoved who had to be carried to his execution in Ryvangen after the torture he had suffered at the hands of the Germans.

Chapter 7

Memories of War

As the years have gone by I have been fascinated how many of my own childhood recollections tie in with documented historical events that I have read or heard about. This confirms the idea that one usually does not realize what is happening while it is happening and that it is hard to see what a building looks like from the inside.

Though more than 60 years have passed since the Germans rolled into my boyhood town, many of the sights and sounds of the Occupation, of the war, remain etched into my memory and are easily recalled in some detail. And though many of those details are filtered through time and the perception of a nine-year-old boy, they still seem as vivid now as they did back then. Here then, in no particular order, are a selection of snapshots of the days and nights that constitute my memory of that time.

ii ii ii

On a sunny summer afternoon, probably in 1944, I was riding a streetcar through an industrial neighborhood on Østerbro. The sidewalks were teeming with people at that time of day. Suddenly a German car pulled up; the occupants poured out, grabbed a man on the sidewalk, and shot him dead with their submachine guns. He looked like ground meat when they were through with him. The Germans got back in their car and drove off. The streetcar and its passengers continued on its way. It probably was a so-called "clearing murder"—when the Resistance executed a Danish collaborator, the Germans or their Danish auxiliaries would sometimes pick a person at random and shoot them in the same locale the next day.

There was a teenage boy in our apartment block who bragged to us younger kids that he was a member of HIPO. We believed that he was either that or an informer. One day the Resistance picked him up and shot him in one of the rear stairways of the building. We were told that the lady in the kitchen next to the stair landing where he was executed heard him plead, "I will never do it again!"

One of my playmates in the same building had two older sisters who had been accused of being *Feltmadrasser* (Field mattresses), an epithet aimed at Danish women who went out with German soldiers, suggesting that, like mattresses, the women had been slept upon. The penalty for cavorting with the invaders was often, as in the case of my friend's sisters, having one's head shaved bald.

One day, soldiers in the garden of Rydhave inadvertently fired some shots. The Gestapo across the street thought they were being attacked and returned fire. A firefight between the two groups of German soldiers erupted across the road. Many of the neighborhood apartment houses ended up pock marked with bullet holes.

Many buildings, including the one in which my grandparents lived, had air raid sirens installed on their roofs. These sirens were tested at noon every day. Air raid alarms sounded frequently as Allied bombers flew over on their way to Germany. But as the planes rarely bombed Danish targets, people tended to ignore them, often sleeping through the alarms and remaining at home rather than running to the air raid shelters. Oddly enough, away from home, where the sirens were not as close, their sound tended to have more of an effect, waking one up from a sound sleep.

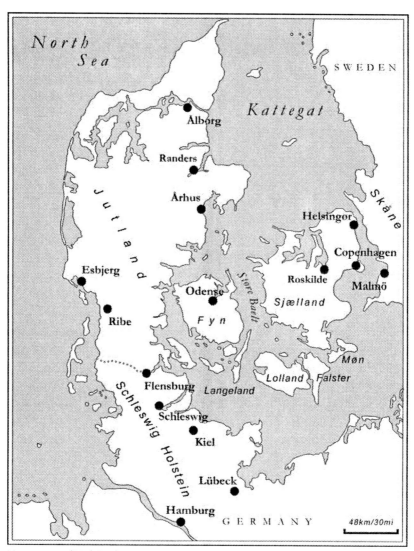

Map courtesy of Mark Tveskov

DENMARK

2. A fashion to which the Germans quickly put a stop. From July 9, 1943, the wearing of a cap with a red circle in the center surrounded by white and blue rings was forbidden. Author's own "RAF hat" is shown below.

3. The author (left), Borge Jensen (rear), and author's cousin, Jan Hedegaard (right), row a dingy at Rødvig, Denmark, summer 1944.

4. At 11:00 a.m. on September 19, 1944, a false air raid alert enables the SS and German police to trap and imprison the Danish police force throughout the country. In Copenhagen, the head offices of the Police Administration are raided and the Germans occupy police headquarters. Many escape, but some 2,000 police officers are conveyed on to ships bound for Germany. The truck above contains Danish policemen being taken away.

5. Soon afterwards, the Germans close off access to the Amalienborg Palace and a battle ensues with Danish police taking up position to defend the king's residence.

6. The plenipotentiary of the Reich, Dr. Werner Best (rt.), accompanied by Prime Minister Erik Scavenius on the occasion of Dr. Best's audience with Crown Prince Frederick on February 6, 1943.

7. A German soldier carrying away Danish goods.

8. Dr. Werner Best saluting fallen German soldiers, the victims of a British air raid on March 21, 1945. The target was Gestapo Headquarters in Shellhuset, Denmark. In addition to the headquarters, many civilian structures were also destroyed, resulting in numerous casualties.

9. Also in attendance at the commemoration for the German victims of the Shellhuset raid is SS General Pancke. Although few Danes knew him by sight, he was the man who signed the German execution orders for Danish citizens during the last year of the war.

10. Soon after the German surrender, a crowd gathers at the site near Ryvangen where the Nazis had executed members of the Danish Resistance and others. Flowers adorn the execution posts in remembrance of the victims.

11. The dog kennels once used for the pets of patrons of the Dagmar Cinema are converted into short-term holding cells by the Gestapo. Prisoners were unable to stand upright and although the time spent within was limited, the discomfort was extreme—both physically and psychologically.

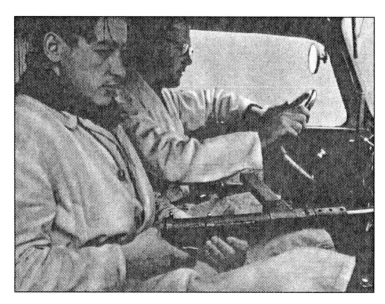

12. Members of the Danish Resistance on their way to commit an act of sabotage against a German target, British Sten gun at the ready.

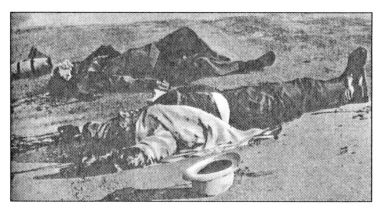

13. Two collaborators/informants killed by the Resistance are left on a quiet residential street in the town of Glostrup.

14 & 15. April 9, 1945. The 5th anniversary of the Occupation is commemorated with 2 minutes of silence by thousands assembled in the Town Hall Square in Copenhagen. But the silence is suddenly broken by gun fire from German "provocateurs" dressed in civilian clothes. People rush for cover in doorways and huddle behind air raid shelters (below). It was the first and only time the newly completed shelters were actually used.

16. Towards the end of the war, thousands of German refugees pour into Denmark, putting a strain on local resources such as food and shelter, and creating problems for Danish citizens.

17. A German refugee "camp" in Copenhagen. In the month of April, 1945, more than a thousand refugees died amid the squalor of such camps in and around greater Copenhagen.

18. Field Marshal Montgomery makes his entry into Copenhagen on Saturday, May 12, 1945. Standing in King Christian X's car, the victorious commander salutes the cheering crowd.

19. The first British dispatch rider to cross the Danish frontier at Krusaa on May 5, 1945, is given a joyful reception by an enthusiastic crowd of newly liberated Danes.

20. Danish collaborators are arrested and taken away to stand trial for treason. Protecting these prisoners from angry Danish crowds was often a difficult and risky task.

21. German soldiers, defeated and stripped of their weapons, leave Denmark on foot, in single file.

22. Saturday, May 5, 1945. Liberation!

"More than two thousand black days of tyranny and barbarity have come to an end and this spring evening will be indelibly imprinted on our consciousness as the hour when peace, freedom and justice again won a foothold on earth. Jubilation is endless over the whole of our country, flags are put out, the tones of the national anthem are heard, and as darkness draws on, lights are lit in all windows." -Ernst Mentze, from *5 Years: The Occupation of Denmark in Pictures*

Copenhagen was bombed twice by the Royal Air Force. The first time was on January 27, 1943; the purpose was to bomb the large Burmeister & Wain shipyards in Christianshavn. My father sat at his desk playing chess with my grandfather. Being paralyzed, my father could not have gone to the building's shelter even if he had wanted to. When the planes came over we shut off the lights and opened the blackout shades. Fires lit up the horizon over Christianshavn and we could see the British bombers flying over our building at low altitude. In the middle of the raid my mother appeared. She had been ordered into a shelter on her way home from work, but left the shelter and ran home instead. As it later turned out, the shipyard was only lightly damaged, but a neighboring sugar factory and an entire residential block were destroyed.

In school we were given flyers that illustrated all the different kinds of bombs being used by the Allies, in case we would find an unexploded sample. The phosphorous bombs were especially scary. I never found any unexploded bombs, but once, on my street, I found pieces of the windshield from an aircraft that had been in a firefight.

The second R.A.F. raid took place March 31, 1945. The R.A.F., using DeHavilland Mosquito bombers, precision-bombed the Shell Oil Company building located in the center of Copenhagen. The Gestapo had requisitioned the Shell House to use as its headquarters and many Danish prisoners were held on its sixth floor. The building was located in the center of Copenhagen next to the railroad tracks that ran in the bottom of what used to be the city moat just north of the main railroad station. Oddly enough, the Germans had camouflaged the building (as if a multistoried square hill that suddenly had appeared in the center of the city would fool anyone!)

The Mosquitoes came in nearly at street level, flying above the railroad tracks. When they reached the building, they pulled up, dropping their bombs in a tactic known as skip bombing. Some of the prisoners, including Mogens Fog, escaped when the incendiary bombs hit the lower floors, but many were killed. One *Mosquito* hit a tall railroad signal mast and crash-landed in a Copenhagen park. Its crew was saved by the Resistance and eventually returned to England. Before the landing the pilot jettisoned his bombs and they hit the Catholic French School on Maglekildevej. Some of the pilot's squadron mates then thought that the school was the target and dropped their bombs on it, killing about a hundred children and nuns who had sought shelter in the interior stairwells of the building only to have the stair towers collapse on them. I was sheltered with my schoolmates in the stairwells of Skovshoved School, about five miles from the target. I had to use the toilet and was allowed to cross the schoolyard for that purpose. It was absolutely quiet, even the birds were silent.

ii ii ii

There were a number of armed confrontations between the Germans and the Danish army on August 29, 1943. As a former member of the *Garderforeningen* (the Danish Royal Guard) my father belonged to an association of members that entitled him to wear a special lapel pin, and on occasion young soldiers would salute him as he sat in his wheel chair. Members of the association would also visit him at home. I was there when he received such a visit after the armed confrontations of August 29, 1943. The man who visited him had been present at the battle between the Germans and the Royal Guard at the barracks on Sølvgade. He told my father that the Danish colonel had been shot in the abdomen and was turned over to the Germans under a flag of truce. The Germans accepted the stretcher, then dumped the wounded officer on the street and kicked him to death.

A serious confrontation took place between the Germans and the people of Copenhagen during an unusually hot June in 1944. As rumor had it, the final straw that triggered the confrontation was that the Germans wanted to use uniforms of the demobilized Danish army for one of their terrorist Danish auxiliary corps. Regardless of whether the rumor was true or not, the Danes did declare a general strike closing all stores and businesses.

I was on summer vacation and staying with my parents on Østerbro. The neighborhood stores did open their back doors to their fellow citizens, so we could obtain food and other necessities. The Germans retaliated by shutting off the gas, electricity, and water to the city. We therefore had to go to the city's parks with buckets to get water. Bathing was not a high priority in those days and we did get some drinking water from the building's idle hot water tanks. My mother and I went to the Kildevælds Park, about four blocks from where we lived on Venøgade street, with our buckets to fetch water. There were strict curfews, but those of us who lived in large apartment blocks could move around in the closed courtyards of those buildings. There were a lot of parties and get-togethers, everyone sharing whatever they had of food, liquor, and cigarettes. Then as now, the Danes took their eating and drinking seriously.

The Germans had moved an artillery battery to the end of Venøgade and fired a shell into an apartment building about a block from ours. I do not know why they did it nor if anyone was hurt, but I do remember the big hole in the building. The Germans eventually announced that unless the strike was over by noon on a certain date, they would shell the city.

The morning of the deadline my mother and I went to a dairy plant on our bicycles and picked up a liter bottle of milk. There were long lines at the plant, but everybody got a bottle of milk. When we got home, it was decided that I should go to my grandparents' home in Skovshoved to be safe. At first the plan was that I was to accompany our neighbors, the Hs, but they could not decide what valuables to take with them, so my mother gave me the bottle of milk and told me to get on the bike and go to my grandmother's home alone, something I had done often under normal circumstances.

So off I went, zigzagging through the German barricades, fascinated by the soldiers lying huddled behind the sandbag barricades with their helmets and machine guns. I arrived safely in Skovshoved, but the milk on the luggage carrier of my bike had curdled from shaking in the heat. I suspect that it did not go to waste, as my grandmother used to prepare a dish that was based on sour milk and covered with pumpernickel crumbs and brown sugar; never one of my favorites.

The strike was eventually settled and the city was not shelled. Neither did the Danish uniforms reappear until after the German surrender.

As an adult and a parent of four children, I have often thought of the agony that my parents went through, having to send their nine-year-old boy away by himself, knowing full well that there was a real possibility that they never would see him again. For me at age nine, however, the experience was one of great adventure and excitement!

Every fifteen or twenty minutes a German patrol plane would cruise up the coast of North Zealand. It was usually a Blohm & Voss 138—a twin-tailed seaplane equipped with three noisy and smoking diesel engines. It was officially named the *Seedrache* (Sea Dragon) but due to its shape it was unofficially called the *Flying Clog*. We called it *Anders And* (Donald Duck). One flew so low one day it knocked the chimney off the apartment building in which my parents lived on Østerbro. Another strange plane used on occasion was called the Heinkel Zwilling. It consisted of two twin-engined Heinkel 111 bombers joined at the wingtips, with a fifth engine mounted at the junction. It was intended to tow gliders, but also used for patrols. It was scary to see this weird, five-engine monster passing overhead at low altitude.

ii ii ii

Although gun battles, fatal to both sides, took place between the Resistance and Germans, the Resistance rarely targeted individual German soldiers. The reprisals were just too costly to the Danish population. However, Danish collaborators were fair game even if the reprisals caused the death of Danish poets, priests and other non-violent celebrities.

Due to the shortage of fuel—mainly coal—most buildings, including the one in which my parents lived, stopped furnishing hot water for the tenants. In my grandparents' building they provided hot water one Saturday each month. On that Saturday my grandparents had many visitors from all over the city.

My grandmother also had use of the building's laundry room on a certain day each month. In those days before the electric washing machine became a common appliance, that meant that she had to fire up a large cauldron of hot water and wash the clothes by hand, hanging them to dry in the same room. There was an old fashioned galvanized bathtub in which we took turns bathing on those washdays.

An alternative was to go to one of Copenhagen's two large public indoor swimming pools. For a low price one was given a small, reusable can of strong, brown liquid soap. After that, one would shower, lather using the soap, and then scrub with excelsior, a packing material made of wood shavings. Next came the two saunas. One was a dry heat room, the other a steam bath. After using one of the two saunas and before going into the big swimming pool, one had to jump into an 8'x 8' ice-cold pool. Then came the big thrill—swimming in the big indoor pool, complete with diving boards! It was a real treat, especially in the winter. As one of these pools was located on Østerbro near my parents' apartment, my mother and I frequently took advantage of this pleasant –and sanitary—excursion.

My mother worked as a switchboard operator in a large office building on the *Rådhuspladsen* (City Hall square) in Copenhagen. One day she received what was then colloquially known as a "telephone bomb"—a phoned-in message that the building would be blown up. This could not be considered an idle threat at that time. The Resistance would sabotage industrial plants that worked for the German war effort, and the Germans in reprisal would blow up civilian targets, such as the concert hall in Tivoli a block from my mother's office.

My mother called her boss, who ordered her to call everyone in the building and tell them to evacuate. Using the old-fashioned switchboard with its many plug-in lines, she did what she was told.

When the job was done, she advised her boss, who then allowed her to leave the building. She had been very calm through this whole process, but when she picked up her personal belongings and put them in her pocketbook, she also "calmly" picked up a full glass of water and started to put it in the pocketbook.

The personnel gathered around the Dragon fountain in front of the city hall and to memorize the occasion had their picture taken by the boss. The next day he presented my mother with a homemade medal: A military style cross made of cardboard and inscribed *Telephone Heroine.*

In 1944 my mother, cousin, and I were on summer vacation in Rødvig in southern Zealand. My uncle, *M,* came to meet us and we traveled together back to Copenhagen. We took the Berlin-Copenhagen express from Næstved. It was composed of both Danish and German carriages. As was normal in 1944, the train was incredibly crowded, but Uncle *M,* being a big shot in the Danish State Railroads, got reserved first class seats for my mother and himself, while my cousin and I were placed in the luggage car. For two adventurous little boys, this was not a hardship!

The car belonged to the Deutsche Reichsbahn, but the train crew was Danish. The Danish attendant opened one of the large sliding doors in the side of the car for us—a really big thrill—threw a couple of mail bags on the floor by the open door, and told us to sit on them. "It is German mail, so it is OK to sit on it," he told us. It was a great train trip.

Chapter 8
Recreation: Entertainment, Toys & Games

Copenhagen was blacked out, but neutral Sweden across the sound was not. We wondered at the lit-up cities of Malmö and Landskrona that beckoned across the water. Yet at home, even the ubiquitous bicycles were affected, with blacked-out lanterns and white-painted fenders.

Movies

In Denmark movie theaters, the rows and seats were numbered and prices varied depending on which row and seat you chose. As row 11 was slightly more expensive than rows 1-10, my grandfather would always purchase the end seats in row 10. The movies were both domestic and foreign with Danish subtitles. Advertisements, previews of coming attractions, and a newsreel always preceded the feature film. Sometimes, if we were lucky, we'd get a cartoon as well.

I remember watching Nelson Eddy sing "Rosemarie, I Love You" to Jeanette McDonald there before the war. But after the invasion, British and American movies could no longer be imported. As a result, the Danish film industry thrived as it had not since the advent of the "talkies." Before the war, Denmark had exported silent movies, even to the U.S. But does anyone remember Asta Nielsen today? As the movies were, of course, censored by the occupiers, the studios had to be quite ingenious in creating topical movies, so most of them were escapist. I do not think that any of the Danish movies produced from 1940 to 1945 survive on their merit in a film library. (It was fun to see the glamorous stars of the war years and my childhood reappear as senior citizens in the Danish movie *Babette's Feast* in the 1990s.)

Many German movies were shown, but my parents and my grandparents did not patronize any of them, nor was I allowed to. So the choice was between Danish and Swedish films. The newsreels were all made by the German *UFA* Studio and could not be avoided, as they were shown before every feature film. They were pretty heavy-handed propaganda.

One of these newsreels showed a fleet of Luftwaffe bombers heading for England and the commentator saying, "All but one returned from the mission." A voice from the Danish audience responded: "Don't worry; it will be back by the 9 o'clock show!"

ii ii ii

Part of my Uncle M's responsibilities at the state railways was the small movie house in the main Copenhagen railroad station called *DSB Kino-Den Vide Verden*, which translates to "The Wide World." But to us kids it sounded a lot like, and therefore was known to us as, *Den Hvide Verden*: "The White World."

As was common in the railroad stations in many large cities in those days, this movie house repeated hour-long programs consisting of newsreels, shorts, and cartoons. The program changed weekly and provided entertainment for waiting passengers. Somehow they managed to show Popeye cartoons right up until Pearl Harbor.

The ticket taker knew who we were and let us in for free, so we would try to catch the new show once a week. This meant my having to travel alone a half dozen miles from Skovshoved to the center, either by bicycle or streetcar.

Somehow Uncle *M* was able to obtain some American films during the war, which he would show to an invited, private audience in this movie house. Uncle M was asking for trouble. At one of these showings I saw *Petrified Forest*, an American movie with Leslie Howard, a Jewish actor. Besides being in an American movie, being Jewish made Leslie Howard *persona non grata* to the Germans. (There is now a 24-hour supermarket in the corner of the station where this movie house used to be.)

Under my uncle's auspices one of the Danish studios produced some sort of Danish propaganda film during the war, probably somehow related to the state railroad and tourism. My cousin and I were both in it. I sat in front of a pea-green door blowing soap bubbles with a clay pipe. My cousin was shown playing with a toy farm and small toy animals. After the shooting we were allowed to keep these props. Years later my mother tried to locate the film, but it had gone the way of all acetate film. So much for my one chance at film stardom.

Radio

Radio was an important source of entertainment, especially during the long, dark Danish winter evenings. There was but one Danish station, the government-run Danish State Radio. The format was fixed and included mostly half-hour cultural programs starting with gymnastics in the morning, followed by a religious service from the Copenhagen cathedral. As the day went on there were concerts with light and classical music and late in the afternoon a half-hour children's program.

The State Radio had its own symphony orchestra and Boys' Choir. The Choir was directed by Henning Elbirk, my homeroom teacher at Gammel Hellerup Gymnasium. News programs were scattered through the day, but we did not pay much attention to them as they were heavily censored. There were many educational programs and several times a week dramatic presentations, often soap opera style serials, carried over from week to week. All these programs seemed to have to have a social message of some sort.

Saturday evening a popular variety program called "Weekend Hytten" (The Weekend Cabin) was broadcast in a format much like Garrison Keillor's "Prairie Home Companion." We rarely missed that program, which featured skits and performances by popular Danish singers and performers. For real news we depended on Swedish radio and BBC's Danish newscast, both of which were forbidden.

All European radios in those days, rather than showing numbers on the dial, showed the names of all the major cities in Europe: Hilversum, Berlin, Prague, Warsaw, Vienna, Belgrade, etc. Many of these cities had been bombed or otherwise destroyed. Those that remained only broadcast German propaganda. All Allied stations were jammed by the Germans and were difficult to hear, even with the illegal homemade antennas that we used. Jamming consisted of a loud "dit-dit-dit-dit" signal broadcast on the same wavelength that made it difficult to hear the broadcast.

News broadcasts by the Danish State Radio were heavily censored and so we depended on Swedish radio and the BBC, when we could get them. A mystery that we always wondered about was the meaning of the coded messages at the end of the BBC broadcasts: "Greetings to Harry, Niels, etc.," We believed they were signals to the Resistance and indicated actions to be initiated or the sites of weapons parachute drops.

Theatre

We often took advantage of live theatre and attended performances at one or more of the venues in Copenhagen. The Royal Theatre featured mainly ballets, which was not of great interest to young boys—at least not this one. My Uncle *M* took us to see the operas *The Merry Widow* and *Die Fledermaus*. The star was Max Hansen, a German who had become a Danish citizen after marrying Britta Sylvester Hvid, a Dane, in 1940. He was born in Mannheim, Germany, grew up in Munich, and made his debut in Denmark in 1914 where he was called "The Little Caruso." Max Hansen spoke, sang, and acted in Danish, but with a charming Viennese accent.

We also put on plays at home with our puppet theatres. The flats and characters were all cut out of printed cardboard, purchased in kits. We especially sought out plays that called for one of the characters to fall through the trap door in the stage.

Very popular were the so-called *Revys* (from the French *revue* and pronounced that way), which usually were shown at one of Copenhagen's two outdoor amusement parks, Tivoli or Bakken, or at one of the numerous cabaret theatres. These shows consisted of a series of live comedy skits and musical numbers, and it was very difficult for the Germans to censor them, as much of the performance was ad-libbed and innuendo. The nuances in the songs and skits in Danish tended to escape the censors, but not the audience, even young children. I once attended a Revy sitting next to a German soldier and his date. He obviously enjoyed the show, but probably did not "get" the skits. I did.

There were many favorite Revy actors, including Helge Kjærulf Smith. In his most famous number he appeared dressed in a ridiculous costume, banging a large pole covered with bells and rattles in time to the music. The refrain of the song was *Mågerne fly'r, taber de no'et? Vi er alle i samme båd!* (The gulls fly over us, what do they drop? We are all in the same boat!) This obviously loses everything in translation, but at the time it was quite poignant and everyone understood the meaning, which was that all of us were suffering equally under the German occupation.

Well-known jazz musicians such as Kai Winding and Svend Asmussen got their starts in the Revys. Asmussen and his partners, Gerda Neumann and her brother, Ulrik, made an international name for themselves in the jazz world of the '40s and '50s. Gerda Neumann was killed in 1947 in the crash of a KLM DC-3 at Kastrup Airport in Copenhagen. The same crash killed the grandson of the king of Sweden, heir to the Swedish throne, and the American singer Grace Moore. Geysendorffer, KLM's chief pilot, piloted the plane. Someone had forgotten to remove the wooden wedges that kept the horizontal and vertical stabilizers from moving in the wind and apparently the captain forgot to check to see if the controls were working. The plane took off, stalled, and crashed

Public Outings

The *Alsang* were enormous gatherings, sing-alongs actually, that took place early in the war during the long, light summer evenings. Thousands of people would gather in the city parks to demonstrate their solidarity and national spirit. There they would picnic and sing patriotic songs.

When the Germans began to periodically impose curfews, *Sammenskudsgilder*, cooperative neighborhood parties, became very popular. Families would gather in rotation in one another's homes and celebrate, everyone contributing something. The unique thing about these gatherings was that they were neighborhood affairs and brought people together, who although living in the same large apartment complexes, really did not know each other well. In the suburbs people would cut holes in the thick hedges that traditionally divide Danish house lots so they could circulate without going out in the streets during curfews. These cuts have long since grown over again.

Despite the fact that the food at these parties was wonderful and often plentiful, the restaurants continued to thrive during the war even though rationing coupons had to be presented for each meal and the wine selections were limited. I suppose that beer and akvavit were still available (otherwise the Germans really would have faced a popular uprising), but that was not really on my radar screen at the time. For us children, restaurants were not often on the program. My mother occasionally would take me to a vegetarian restaurant upstairs in a back alley off Strøget, however, which I remember as pleasant events.

In Copenhagen there were, and still are, two well-known amusement parks: Tivoli, located in the center of the city, and Dyrehavsbakken, normally known as just Bakken, in Klampenborg north of the city. Tivoli mixed popular entertainment with classical music and beer halls with fancy restaurants thus providing something for everybody. It seemed that everyone would traditionally go to Tivoli at least once each summer and for us children it was definitely a highlight of the season. In an act of terrorism, the Germans eventually bombed Tivoli, destroying its concert hall and much of its priceless collection of sheet music. This was in reprisal for some act of sabotage. The park was immediately rebuilt and did not lose its atmosphere, even if those of us who knew it before could tell the difference. We wondered, for example, what became of the merry-go-round with the real miniature Nimbus motorbikes that we used to ride? Nimbus was a brand of four cylinder Danish motorcycles with chain drive made by Nielsen & Fisker, a manufacturer of vacuum cleaners known as Nilfisk (Fish of the Nile). Nilfisk later branched out worldwide making industrial vacuum cleaners with absolute filters used in asbestos removal.

Bakken was located near a race track in the woods north of Copenhagen and had more of a beer hall atmosphere than Tivoli—but also with a much more exciting roller coaster than Tivoli's rather tame one! In a word only a Dane understands, Bakken was *folkelig*—a concept that has something to do with the whole idea of social equality, but tending towards the lowest common denominator. There was no attempt at culture at Bakken, no concert hall, but lots of shooting galleries, fortune tellers, and beer gardens with not only good beer, but also good food—an absolute must in Denmark. It was a fun place to visit during a summer evening and, like Tivoli, such a visit would happen at least once a summer—unless cousins visited from "the provinces" and we would have an excuse to go again.

Something that nearly every public event—from attending concerts to waiting for the streetcar—had in common was the need to stand in line. We stood in line for almost everything. And in so doing, a type of unwritten law evolved that determined our behavior while in line. It was called *køkultur*, which literally translated means "queue etiquette" or "the culture of standing in line." For example, one did not "cut in," push, or otherwise behave in other than an orderly fashion. As to why it evolved, I can only speculate that it had something to do with the Danish tradition of property in as much as there was less a feeling of "we vs. them" when it came to the government and its many rules and regulations. For example, many Danes have difficulty in understanding why Americans itemize their tax deductions. They think it is crazy to do so as they accept their exorbitant income taxes as "their" taxes, not the government's. Whatever the reason, *køkultur* was prevalent, accepted, and made standing in line a tolerable experience.

Vacations

While few people owned summer houses, it seems that everyone traditionally would go away for at least a week at the shore each summer. We would either rent a cottage or stay at a *pension*—a boarding house where food and lodging were included. This tradition continued during the war, but transportation became more of a challenge. If the cottage was located too far to reach by bicycle, we would ride our bikes to the main station in Copenhagen, put them on a train, pick them up at the nearest station to the vacation destination, and ride the bikes to our pension or cottage. Once in a while we would be taken from the local station to the cottage in a horse drawn wagon, especially exciting for us city kids.

The days would be spent at the beach—even if it rained, which it does a lot in Denmark. So we would bundle up. Few kids wore bathing suits till they got up in their early teens, but there was no public adult nudity on the beaches in those days. Everyone learned how to change into and out of their bathing suits right on the beach under a terry cloth bathrobe of some sort. This is a custom that all Danes learn to do discreetly and well, and which ranks right up there with learning to eat with a knife and fork (knife in the right hand, the fork in the left) as a rite of passage into responsible adulthood. (All of the above notwithstanding invading Germans, of course!)

I would also usually spend a week in the parsonage of St.Peter's Church in Slagelse with my Uncle O, the Lutheran minister, Aunt I, his wife, and my five cousins—two girls, three boys. The two girls were older and the boys younger than I was, but I was closest to the older girl cousin, Hanne, who was five years my elder.

The parsonage had a large beautiful garden and a little grove of full-grown trees. Hanne and I built tree houses and played war or "Cowboys and Indians." We also had to go to church on Sunday and weed and pick vegetables in the garden. At least once a week the whole bunch of kids would be put in an enormous wooden tub and thoroughly scrubbed down by my aunt. All of this was fun as well as, I suppose, character building, as it taught me, an only child, how to function in a large family that did not live in a city apartment.

Next to the big house, my uncle and cousins had dug a real trench and underground air raid shelter—just in case. Again, getting to the parsonage was a challenge, as we never did know if the trains would run on time or run at all. Once aboard it was great fun, even if the trains were extremely crowded and one got cinders in one's eyes when poking one's head out the compartment window.

Toys & Games

My grandfather used to make most of my toys, as well as my cousin's. He would carve cars and trains out of wood and use the pre-war copper coins for wheels. Cars usually would have one *øre* wheels, while locomotives would use the larger five *øre* coins for the drivers. The scale of these small masterpieces was close to that of the prewar British-made Dinky Toy cars. I would leave a drawing of the kind of car I desired, usually a real car, such as a Ford or Opel, and after many protestations about my having too many cars already, it would be waiting for me when I came home from school the next day. I still have a few of these cars and occasionally one turns up in a cousin's or nephew's childhood collection.

As a teenager, he apprenticed as a pattern maker in a foundry and there learned how to make exacting wooden models including beautiful ships carved with his pocketknife. When we would visit the harbor at Skovshoved, he would quickly whittle a rudimentary hull out of a piece of scrap wood, mount a mast and a long rudder, and under a simple paper sail, the little ship would set off for the impossible goal of the Swedish coast. The flat wooden sticks used in ice cream bars made perfect rudders.

He made very imaginative toy guns for us, too. One not to be forgotten was an "elephant gun" with a barrel made from a broken picnic table umbrella, to be used for our imaginary safaris. Another masterpiece in realism was a Husquarna submachine gun. These homemade martial toys were supplemented after the Liberation with real items, such as a Russian .38 revolver—sans firing pin—that I received as a gift from a detective friend. I eventually traded this revolver for a real Winchester bolt-action '22 rifle, which was illegal under both Danish and German law.

To achieve realism in our games we all had to have real steel helmets to wear. German helmets were reasonably easy to obtain and could be repainted with the letters of the various resistance groups—just like the real resistance fighters did after the Liberation. Some of the flat English helmets were around, but were very rare, and quite a few of the unique Danish army helmets were available too. I traded cigarettes with a resistance guard at Ryvangen for a German helmet. When I brought it home my grandmother boiled it and its leather sweatband for hours on the stove, to do away with any German germs that might still lurk within. It went through several incarnations over the years, first in my possession and later in that of my Danish nephews, but was finally brought to the U.S. in the '70s and restored by me to its original German configuration.

Other odds and ends of real uniforms and equipment added to the realism of our games. At some point my grandfather expanded into making simple crossbows that we would use for target practice in his garage that, in addition to housing the Vauxhall, was his workshop.

We had store-bought toys, too; mainly small cars and ships. Before the war most of these cars were Dinky Toys made by Meccano in Great Britain or Märklin toys from Germany. Both Meccano and Märklin also made their versions of the American Erector sets, as well as very expensive, but beautifully made HO gauge electric trains. After the occupation, English toys disappeared from the market and we were discouraged from getting German toys. Depending on one's family's political inclination, this was easily enforced by them, as they obviously held the purse strings.

Into this void jumped Tekno, the Danish toy manufacturer. Tekno began by manufacturing its own version of the Erector sets and then branched into toy trucks made of sheet metal in approximately "O" scale. These trucks, which all represented emergency vehicles, were modeled on the pre-war General Motors British Bedford truck and could be completely disassembled. One could thus mix-and-match and, depending on how many trucks one had and how many pieces one had not lost, create one's own fleet. Tekno then began manufacturing vehicles in the same scale as Dinky and Märklin, initially using the 1938 U.S. Ford truck chassis as the base for a variety of different vehicles. Later came a 1940 Packard ambulance and eventually Danish Triangel fire trucks. Due to the shortage of rubber even for tires for toy cars, the cars made during the war had wheels realistically made of sheet metal stampings. After the war rubber tires were used.

These small cast cars were meticulously modeled on the originals and solid enough to be used by little boys. After the war they became the basis for Tekno's competition with Dinky and Corgy in the international market, an effort that regrettably petered out in the '70s when the firm went out of business.

Tekno also manufactured small toy airplanes. They made three kinds: The Boeing B-17 (based on an early version, the B-17C); the Douglas SBD dive-bomber; and the British Blenheim twin-engine bomber. Tekno also made a model of the Danish-built twin engine KZ-IV ambulance plane in a slightly larger scale.

The planes bore British and U.S. markings and that upset the Germans. The owner of Tekno was arrested and imprisoned. He was eventually released after agreeing to equal representation for German aircraft. So now one could purchase such unlikely planes as B-17s, SBDs and Blenheims with German and Italian, as well as with Swedish and Red Cross markings. Like the Germans' ban on the RAF caps in 1943, this was a Pyrrhic victory for them, as it made them look pretty silly. It was not too difficult to scrape the German markings off the toy planes, assuming that one's parents ever would buy a plane with German markings on it in the first place. They were rarities indeed, but someone did give me a black "German" B-17 that I reconditioned with silver paint and American markings.

A series of small, relatively inexpensive toy plastic airplane models came from Germany, probably made by Wiking. The Luftwaffe had originally used them as recognition models, but someone had the bright idea of marketing them as toys. They depicted German, British, American, and Italian models, and were quite detailed and also quite fragile.

In addition to Tekno's products, Pilot, another Danish firm, made small toy ships in about 1:800 scale. These were also models of real ships and ran the gamut from cargo ships through ocean liners to all kinds of warships from all nations. For some reason there did not appear to be a stigma attached to buying the models of real German warships (the beautiful one of the German battleship *Gneisenau* was especially desirable), maybe because one could create a "real" sea battle while playing. We called these little ships *blyskibe*, or lead ships, as they were made of some sort of a soft lead-zinc alloy. As this alloy deteriorates when the zinc leaches out, they literally crumble away over the years. Thus any surviving samples are of great value today. The earliest samples in the collection I had then had little wire masts and booms, which my parents removed to prevent us kids from getting poked by them. The Pilot Company till recently was still in business, making promos for shipping lines.

From Germany came Lineol and Elastolin toy soldiers, Indians, and cowboys in all kinds of belligerent poses. The figures were made of a material that basically was glue and sawdust cast in molds. They too are quite valuable today; few have survived, as they eventually would dissolve in the humid Danish climate. Lineol made figures of Hitler, Dönitz, and Mussolini, complete with moving arms for the Nazi salute. They also made King Christian X on his horse. A certain proportion of the soldiers were made as British, French, and Italian troops. (Again, what good are toy soldiers if you do not have an enemy?) They had different heads and helmets, but although the uniforms were appropriately painted, they were still the German uniforms under the paint job. I converted all of mine to Allied soldiers by carving the German helmets into the flat British helmets and repainting the bodies myself. Somehow I had obtained a surgical scalpel that was excellent for this microsurgery

Before the Danish "Lego" blocks, we had small bricks made of baked clay in many configurations. Limited only by one's imagination and number of bricks on hand, all kinds of structures could be built, just like with today's Legos.

Unfortunately the bricks were quite fragile and could not tolerate any kind of moisture, so attrition was significant. A friend of mine while home sick built a model of the locks of the Panama Canal with these blocks in his room and filled it with water. The subsequent disastrous flood made him very unpopular with his mother.

While not intended as a toy, Uncle M brought a very detailed scale model of a FW-200 Condor airliner, about two-foot long, back from a business trip to Berlin. He claimed to have salvaged it from a bombed-out Lufthansa sales office and it was painted in the colors of that company, complete with swastika flag on the tail. He had it professionally repainted in the colors of the Danish Air Line, that flew two of these four-engine airliners. Although it was too big for good playing, my cousin Jan and I did play with it. The tail wheel of the plane was the same as that on a small Märklin motorcycle and sidecar that I had at the time. Years later my cousin had the model professionally restored and it now hangs in the hallway of his house in Denmark.

My cousin also had a Märklin HO gauge electric train set that over the next fifty years grew into a room-sized layout. The original 1930s locomotive and rolling stock are exhibited in a glass case in his living room in Espergærde. Due to the rationing of electricity we usually would dispense with the locomotives and push the cars around the track!

Whether normal for little boys or more topical at the time, most of our games had to do with the war. Even those of our games that would start out in a peaceful scenario eventually all ended in war. We would set up a city, using magazines as the city blocks, and run bus routes through this imaginary city, only to have to reroute these bus routes when the Germans blocked certain streets, as happened in real life. When groups played together we were pragmatic enough to take turns as the Good Guys—the Resistance—and the Bad Guys—the Germans!

My cousin and I, as well as most of our friends, were in the Boy Scouts. Some of us were more enthusiastic than others, but for me it was an exciting experience. My cousin did not care much for it, but was more or less forced to join by his father, my uncle M. Nearly all our Boy Scout leaders were in the Resistance, or claimed to be—especially after the surrender. However, our training was militarily oriented and we knew that we were being trained as a junior militia. While not really games, everything we did in the Boy Scouts was directed toward martial purposes. It was not disguised that all our activities and field exercises had to do with carrying out military goals against some enemy in one form or another. The only missing items were the weapons, but somehow we were familiar with them too.

Chapter 9
Transportation

Once on the beach at Charlottenlund near Skovshoved my cousin and I saw a large group of German soldiers drive onto the beach in their VW "Schwimmwagens." They removed their uniforms and went swimming off the small amphibious jeep-type vehicles. Several of them were covered with what appeared to be insect bites.

Up until the 1960s few people in Denmark had private automobiles. One reason was that the Social Democrat governments considered automobiles luxury items completely out of reach of the ordinary citizen and taxed them heavily. Right after the war American cars became very popular. Because of their large chrome grilles they were dubbed *Dollargrin* (Dollar Grins), but it was next to impossible for a private person to obtain the hard currency with which to purchase such a car. As many Danes had relatives in the U.S., and these relatives wanted to return and visit Denmark after the war, the Danes would purchase their relatives' tickets in Danish Kroner, the relatives would bring their American car with them, and at the end of the visit "give" it to their Danish hosts. The government soon caught on and decided to put an end to this gimmick. A tax of 150% on the *new* value of such "gift cars" was imposed.

My grandfather was one of the relatively few Danes who early on owned a car. In the 1920s he purchased a Willys Overland open touring car that he used in his business to visit the cities and towns where his customers, the commercial fishermen, lived and worked. After the Willys Overland, he had a 1929 Nash four-door sedan with wooden spoke wheels that he kept until he retired, trading it soon afterwards for a 1938 Vauxhall 10.

Along with his father and brother, my grandfather had manufactured single cylinder, two cycle semi-diesel marine engines of his own design named, appropriately, the *Hein* engine. He was always intrigued by new designs and ideas, one of them being the overhead valve engine design. Both the Nash and the Vauxhall were ahead of their times in many ways and both had overhead valve (OHV) engines. The Vauxhall was a British-built General Motors product with a four-cylinder OHV engine and had many modern features. It had a torsion bar suspension, concealed running boards, and "idiot lights" rather than gauges. In fact, the first English words I learned were *Oil* and *Amp* from the idiot lights in my grandfather's car!

Although I do not remember riding in the Nash, there are quite a few photographs of my family and me standing by that car, including one with me sitting on the radiator. But I do remember the Vauxhall.

It was dark blue with royal blue leather upholstery. It had a metal sunroof and the rear window could be covered by a retractable, spring loaded roll-up shade operated remotely by a string from the driver's seat. The car did not have a heater, so in the cold weather we sat wrapped in wool blankets. I remember the smell of the leather upholstery and my grandfather's meticulous maintenance of the car. Eating or drinking in it was absolutely forbidden.

My Uncle O also had a car, but he sold it when the Occupation began, which left the garage in the barn of the parsonage empty. The garage was soon rented out and a 1938 Opel Olympia stored there—another General Motors product, this one built in Germany. It was very much like the Vauxhall under the skin, but with a different body altogether. I liked the sleeker and more modern appearance of the Opel better than that of the Vauxhall, but my grandfather told me that he preferred the Vauxhall because you could not see its differential from the rear. He said that the Opel's "slip was showing."

Although my grandfather's car was grounded and its license plates turned in, he would start it up on occasion, cranking it by hand to save the battery. As gasoline was unavailable, he would buy a liter of benzene in the local pharmacy and use that for fuel. Once he got it started, he would back the car the one car length out of the garage the distance to the gate permitted and drive it back in. It was a great treat the neighborhood kids and me to be invited to take this ride, which took but a few seconds in each direction.

Only physicians, ambulances, and other emergency vehicles were allowed to use gasoline, and most gasoline stations were closed altogether. Except for the electrically powered trolley buses all the bus lines operating within Copenhagen eventually were shut down.

This was somewhat of a hardship for our family as there was no other direct public transportation between Skovshoved, where I lived with my grandparents, and Gentofte where my cousin lived. Stephansen's Rutebiler, a private company, operated the bus line on that route, using brand new German Büssing-NAG buses with bodies built in Denmark by Dansk Automobilbyggeri (DAB). At the beginning of the occupation they equipped their buses with wood burning gas generators, but eventually ceased operation till after the war. Under the agreement between Sweden's Count Folke Bernadotte and Germany's SS Reichsführer Heinrich Himmler, some of this company's buses were painted white and used by the Swedish Red Cross in early 1945 to transport Danish and Norwegian prisoners from German concentration camps to Sweden before the end of hostilities.

The trucks, buses, taxis, and commercial vehicles that still operated were equipped with wood burning stoves, the so-called gas generators. Bags full of small blocks of wood were kindled in these stoves, the incomplete combustion creating carbon monoxide that was used as fuel for the engine. Most taxi and truck drivers came to look like stokers, as they had to periodically stoke their stoves and haul the ashes. The manufacture of these gas generators became a thriving industry in Denmark, and many were exported and used in Germany, including by the German military.

Some trucks, vans, and even taxis had their engines removed and were converted to horse drawn wagons. One of the local bakeries in Skovshoved used such a converted small English van, probably an Austin or Morris, for deliveries. The windshield was tilted up and the horse's reins passed through the front window to the driver inside. It would clip-clop down our street.

Like most little boys, I was interested in cars. Most vehicles on the road belonged to the German military, so those were the ones we got to know. The majority of the German military trucks were Opel "Blitz" manufactured at General Motors' most modern European truck factory located at Rüsselsheim in eastern Germany, although some were assembled at GM's Danish assembly plant. Others were Fords manufactured in Germany and France. The Fords even used the same sheet metal as their American 1941 V8 counterpart. The director of Opel's truck plant was Heinz Nordhoff, who after the war would put *Volkswagen* on the map.

The British left many British Bedford trucks at Dunkirk, in Greece, and at Tobruk in North Africa. The Germans repainted them and used them. Like the Opel, they too were Chevrolet clones under the sheet metal.

The standard German army staff car was the straight six Opel Kapitän. It had a Chevrolet engine and a beautiful body designed before the war for a small Cadillac that was never put into production. If I ever saw a Mercedes staff car, as customary in Hollywood movies, I do not remember it. The German officers drove General Motors products. Civilian Volkswagen Beetles were not mass produced till after the war, but the German military used quite a few VW Kübelwagen jeeps and amphibious Schwimmwagens.

Although we saw many German military cars and trucks on the roads, the usual means of transportation for the Danes in those days were bicycles, streetcars, and trains. With the exception of my grandmother, we all had bicycles and used them year-round at all times of the day, except in snow. Fortunately, heavy snow is not common in Denmark, where rain is a much more common feature of the climate in both summer and winter.

Rubber was strictly rationed and it was very difficult to obtain new tires when the old ones wore out. Like everyone else's, my bike had at various times tire patches made of sections of old tires or even twine wrapped around the worn spots on the tires. Ersatz tires made of recycled rubber on a cellulose casing were available, but they did not stand up for long as the cellulose dissolved in water. Some people used wooden "tires" or even tires made of corks strung together around the flange of the wheel, which were noisy and not very satisfactory.

My mother's bicycle was stolen and its frame eventually recovered from Copenhagen harbor by the police, completely stripped. (For that very reason we all memorized the serial numbers of our bikes.) It was a disaster for her as she used the bicycle for both work and recreation. She did get a replacement, but the tires on her brand new bicycle were of very low quality. My father had an invalid tricycle that he could propel with his arms until he lost their use and had to be pushed.

Just before the war the *Kjøbenhavns Sporveie* (Copenhagen streetcar system) had put into service a series of new, longer streetcars that rode on two, four-wheeled bogies. Many of the streetcars were still the old, short four wheeled units dating back to the 1910s or even earlier. As maintenance became a problem, a number of the old streetcars were scrapped, but their motors and four wheeled undercarriages were reused under an attractive new body. We called them *Sparevogne*, a play on words in Danish (*Spare* = to save and *Sporvogn* = streetcar). As the war wore on, the streetcar schedules were heavily curtailed and one had to wait a long time for one to arrive. Once aboard, they would always be very crowded. They were, like everything else, blacked out at night and as the Danish winter nights were very long, one had to depend on the conductor's announcement to know when to get off.

Service also was hindered by long detours caused by the Germans having permanently blocked traffic on all streets bordering the buildings that they had occupied. For instance, today's Hans Christian Andersen's Boulevard (then known as Vestre Boulevard) and Jernbanegade, located at the Northwest corner of Copenhagen's City Hall Square, were blocked with chest-high permanent concrete barriers to protect the SS headquarters in Dagmarhus. The German soldiers patrolled these barriers constantly, but a graffiti artist did manage to write: "Han har ingen bukser på" (He has no pants on) on one of them. It took the guards a while to realize the reason for the chuckles of the passersby.

Railroad service deteriorated as the war went on. The equipment wore out and when the Resistance sabotaged the railroad lines, the Germans, in reprisal, would often blow up civilian passenger trains. Coal for the locomotives was imported from Germany and that supply was quickly drying up. One of my recurring childhood memories is of standing on a cold, dark railroad platform alone or with adults, waiting for a train that at best was overcrowded or late or, at worst, never arrived.

All Danish oil-burning ships were laid up, but coal burning passenger ships continued to sail between the capital and the provinces, and between Copenhagen and Oslo. As coal grew scarcer and the maintenance of the ships declined for lack of spare parts, service grew more and more restricted.

Because of the danger of mines, the ships eventually only sailed in the daytime. Many Danish cargo ships were lost during the war. Many were sunk while sailing for the Allies and several of the vital railroad ferries across the Great Belt (the strait between the main Danish islands of Zealand and Funen) hit mines. In 1948 the old DFDS steamship, the S/S *Kjøbenhavn* sailing between Copenhagen and Aalborg in Northern Jutland, hit a stray mine at night and sank with great loss of life. My mother and I had sailed on her from Copenhagen to Aalborg the year before, and on my way to Scotland during the summer of 1948 I saw her where she laid, just the top of her superstructure jutting out of the water.

Danish Air Lines (DDL, later a partner with the Swedish and Norwegian national airlines in SAS) continued to operate international flights to Berlin, Vienna, and Sweden during most of the occupation. Before the war, DDL operated two JU-52s, two Focke Wulf FW-200 Condors, and a few high-wing, three-engine Fokker airliners. Their schedules were coordinated with those of Lufthansa.

In those days we knew the names and registration letters of the Danish aircraft; after all, there were not that many of them. The Danish airliners were painted completely orange with lots of large Danish flags on the fuselage and wings, as Denmark officially was neutral or at least a non-belligerent. It was fun for us kids to see one of those orange planes flying overhead and, as there were so few of them, to guess which one it was.

One of DDL's FW-200 Condors happened to be in London on April 9, 1940, and was confiscated by the British Royal Air Force. Photographs exist of this plane being test flown in RAF camouflage by its Danish crew. It was useful to the RAF as the military version of the FW-200, known as the Courier, was used by the Luftwaffe as long-range reconnaissance and bombers over the Atlantic to track and bomb the Allied convoys. Unfortunately, it crashed during a landing and was scrapped.

The Danish emergency service, Zonen, was permitted to continue flying ambulance planes to the Danish islands. One model being used was the KZ-IV, a twin engined plane designed and built in Denmark by Kramme & Zeuten. Only two were built; both survive in museums.

Civilians with business in Germany, the occupied European countries, and Sweden continued to travel by conventional means, usually by trains transported by ferry to Sweden and Germany, or by land through Jutland. As it was necessary to obtain permission from the Danish Foreign Ministry and the German authorities, such travel was heavily restricted and controlled. Danish cargo vessels sailing in the Baltic were able to put into Swedish ports for repairs and thus provided yet another contact between the two worlds.

ii ii ii

People left the country illegally in various ways during the Occupation. In one unique case, a couple of enterprising Danish private pilots managed to get their grounded DeHavilland Tiger Moth biplane off the ground and fly it at wave-top level across the North Sea to England. The more prosaic method for travelers who, for whatever illegal reason had to leave the country, was in small boats to Sweden, either as guests of the Resistance or by paying local fishermen. No legitimate refugee was ever denied passage across the Øresund for lack of funds.

This means of transportation evolved as the years went by and became quite well organized, but involved obvious dangers. The Germans patrolled the Øresund between Denmark and Sweden with patrol boats and planes, and even the Swedes were not always completely cooperative. On the other hand, there were reported cases of the German naval patrols turning a deaf ear and allowing refugee boats to continue after having been boarded and inspected.

Another method used was to book passage on the overnight boat between Copenhagen and the Danish island of Bornholm in the Baltic. As the boat at night passed through the canal that separates the Swedish peninsula of Falsterbo from the Swedish mainland, the people would jump overboard and swim ashore. This method involved sneaking an extra passenger aboard, as to prevent this method of escape the passengers were carefully counted on boarding and leaving the ship. The Germans eventually ordered the Danish ships to stop using the canal and go around the Falsterbo peninsula.

Once in Sweden the refugees would either stay there as internees or, if important enough to the war effort, book passage to Great Britain via British Overseas Airlines (BOAC, today British Air). BOAC flew unarmed twin-engine DeHavilland Mosquito bombers and four-engine Handley Page Halifax bombers between Sweden and Great Britain. They were camouflaged, sporting British civilian registrations instead of the R.A.F. roundels on the wings and fuselage. As they flew at very high altitudes and were not pressurized, the passengers had to wear oxygen masks. A famous passenger on one of these flights was the famous Danish nuclear scientist Niels Bohr, who was Jewish and for that reason had to flee the country. Professor Bohr had a rather large face and found the oxygen mask uncomfortable. They say he removed it and slept all the way across Denmark and the North Sea. On landing in England there was quite a lot of concern that this famous man had suffered brain damage on the trip. He had not and went on to do important work on the Manhattan Project in the U.S.

The Germans also flew civilian routes, including a daily flight from Berlin to Oslo via Copenhagen and Malmö in Sweden. Lufthansa used captured Dutch KLM DC-3s on this route, painted in standard civilian Lufthansa colors: silver with a blue line beginning on the blue nose and running along the window line, with the German national flag—a large red banner with a black swastika in a white circle—on the tail. The engine nacelles were painted black.

Both British and German planes had to pass through airspace controlled by the other side to reach Sweden. To my knowledge none of these planes was ever shot down. One can guess that some sort of a gentlemen's agreement must have been in effect, especially so, since German civilian airliners were shot down by the Allies while flying over continental Europe, as were Allied airliners shot down by the Germans while flying over the Channel and the Atlantic.

Chapter 10
Liberation

One evening the city allowed all the neon signs in the City Hall Square to be turned on for the first time in five years. It seemed that the entire city turned up for that event. It was a magnificent sight even though some of them flickered, were not quite completely lit, and faltered, and even if it was only for one evening. The five-year nightmare was over.

I had just returned from a Boy Scout meeting the evening of May 4, 1945, and was listening to the News in Danish from the BBC with my mother and grandparents. The announcer was going over the rather confusing news of the day.

The German army was in full retreat to the west from the Soviets, trying desperately to reach the lines of the western allies to avoid capture and the Soviets' justifiable retribution. The Soviets were rushing northwest toward the Jutland peninsula and were only stopped by field marshal Montgomery's British army's rush across Schleswig-Holstein. Rumors were reported on the broadcast of Soviet paratroopers landing on the southern Danish islands.

I must admit that I only know the details of this broadcast because I have a copy of it. Using wax phonograph discs, a solitary Danish amateur, on his own initiative and at his own expense and risk, had routinely recorded all the BBC news broadcasts. The BBC purchased the collection, the broadcast was reissued fifty years later in 1995, and I was able to obtain a VHS copy.

That being said, I will never forget when the announcer hesitated and then continued with the special bulletin from Field Marshal Montgomery's headquarters announcing the surrender of the German forces in Holland, Northeast Germany, and Denmark, effective at 8 am, May 5, 1945.

Just writing these lines brings back the emotions felt that evening 57 years ago by that ten-year-old boy. Our first reaction, like that of all the neighbors, was to tear down the blackout curtains and light candles in the windows. We then all rushed into the street where someone had lit a bonfire of blackout curtains.

Living close to the homes of the two top German commanders, SS general Dr. Werner Best, the German plenipotentiary and Governor of Denmark, and his neighbor across the shore road, SS General Günther Pancke, head of the Gestapo, the next reaction was to go their houses. There was a covered streetcar stop close to Pancke's house. Graffiti by a German soldier had been written on its wall several days before: "Kameraden, wir haben den Krieg verloren" (Comrades, we have lost the War).

As a mob of people milled about in front of the homes of the two hated men, whose invaders had controlled our lives and deaths for five years, a German Blohn & Voss 138 patrol seaplane flew low overhead and began firing its machine guns. For all we knew, the Luftwaffe was firing their guns in celebration, but discretion being the better part of valor, we went home.

The next morning my mother and I took the streetcar from Skovshoved to the Rådhuspladsen (City Hall Square) in Copenhagen where her office was located. It was a beautiful sunny spring day. The Rådhuspladsen was definitely the center of all the celebrations that day and for quite a few days afterwards. We could go up on the building's roof and observe everything from the corner of Vesterbrogade and what is today known as H. C. Andersen's Boulevard. (This is the spot where the Copenhagen Corner restaurant is now located. Then it was the home of the Frascati restaurant and a Ford dealership.)

The square itself was full of euphoric people, waving Danish flags and singing and greeting the members of the Resistance who appeared all over the city. They were heavily armed, wearing civilian clothes, but they also wore the red-white-blue armband. On their heads they had steel helmets of all types painted with the names of their groups: BOPA, Holger Danske, etc. Danish army officers and police were also about in the uniforms that we had not seen for too long a time.

While standing on the roof of the building, we suddenly had to dodge bullets from a firefight that had erupted at the central Copenhagen police station three or four blocks away, where the Danish Gestapo auxiliaries were resisting. My mother and I eventually left her office and headed down *Strøget*, the series of streets that eventually became the world's first pedestrian shopping mall. At a corner, a couple of Resistance men politely told us to get out of the way, as they were shooting it out with some Danish traitors in a building down the side street.

We reached Kongens Nytorv, the formal square at the end of *Strøget* where the French embassy, the Royal Theatre, the great department store, Magasin du Nord, and the expensive Hotel D'Angleterre were located. The D'Angleterre was used during the war by German officers and other VIPs who never changed the name.

At the beginning of the Nyhavn canal there are underground public toilets. We took advantage of the facilities and then continued down Bredgade toward the Royal Palace. We heard shooting behind us and found out later that right after our departure, several people had been shot in a firefight at the entrance to the underground toilets. It is not clear to me whether it was on this day or the next that we saw the old king and queen crossing City Hall Square in their open Cadillac touring car.

The streetcars stopped running later in the afternoon and we made our way on foot toward my parents' apartment on Østerbro. As we approached the neighborhood, still euphoric and carrying our Danish flags, we noticed that no one was on the street and that people were lurking in the doorways. We soon learned the reason why.

Apparently, the German naval units in Northern Germany, Holland, and Denmark were not instructed to surrender on May 5, which left a couple of naval units in limbo. The German cruiser Nürnberg in Copenhagen refused to surrender to the Danish Resistance and, after a series of tragic misunderstandings, shelled parts of Østerbro on that day. Most people in the neighborhood had spent the time in the air raid shelters, shelters that had seen little use during the occupation. The shelling continued until a cease fire agreement was reached and the German captain agreed to stay quiet until the final surrender came about on May 7th, with his ship guarded by Danish Resistance troops on the pier.

In the following days I returned again and again to the vantage point on the corner of the roof of my mother's office building. From there I saw the first British troops parading through and Field Marshal Montgomery's triumphant entry. The king had placed his own Cadillac open touring car at "Monty's" disposal, as he rode through town to the Royal Palace.

¨¨ ¨¨ ¨¨

A large, albeit peaceful, mob gathered in front of Dagmarhus, the SS headquarters, on the northwest corner of the square. The Germans were busy destroying records preparing to leave the building and its horrible secrets. This was the building where many Danes were tortured and condemned to death in secret German trials. The German leaders had hurriedly vacated their sumptuous offices, leaving half-empty wine bottles and glasses on the tables. A group of male and female Russian slaves were found in the building living on straw mattresses in crowded rooms.

The German soldiers were ordered by field marshal Montgomery to leave the country immediately and walk home. Long lines of defeated and demoralized soldiers were clogging the roads out of Copenhagen on their way to Germany, dropping their weapons by the roadside. The Resistance had issued strict orders to the population to avoid confrontations and leave the Germans alone. To my knowledge there were no confrontations and the Danes still succeeded in ignoring the German soldiers on this last day. Those German soldiers who did show themselves on the streets in the line of duty wore Red Cross armbands.

The Danes who had served as German auxiliaries in the infamous uniformed HIPO, Sommer, and Schalburg Corps, as well as in a number of terrorist gangs, could not leave. They had to either give up or fight it out with the Resistance. If captured they were paraded through the streets on foot or on open trucks. Many other collaborators were also arrested and publicly humiliated. Unfortunately, a number of innocent people were caught up in this net too.

The British paratroopers were overwhelmed by the welcome they received. It became an instant fad to collect their autographs, and their badges and berets became envied souvenirs, especially the unique British paratrooper beret badge that all we kids coveted. A local entrepreneur soon made copies of these wings and sold them to us. The Danish authorities had to put out bulletins imploring the citizens not to take the soldiers' berets or other uniform items as souvenirs, as they supposedly had to pay to replace them out of their own pockets.

※ ※ ※

As the end of the war drew near, Field Marshal Montgomery's British army moved quickly across Schleswig-Holstein to the Baltic coast, isolating the German armies in Denmark and Norway, but more importantly—as it turned out— preventing the fast moving Soviet armies from occupying Denmark. Had that happened, my life history would have been considerably different, as the popular Communist resistance groups in Denmark were ready and willing to take over the country on its "liberation" by the Soviets.

When the announcement finally came of the German surrender, the Danish Resistance took over law enforcement and successfully pleaded with the public for calm. The German troops were allowed to walk home to Germany. Many identified war criminals were arrested and/or intercepted at the border where German soldiers were stripped of everything but their uniforms, and rank and unit insignia were removed from those.

Vast numbers of arms, bicycles, and vehicles piled up at the border. Prior to reaching the border many of the soldiers dropped their weapons along the roadside where anyone could and did pick them up. To this day many Danish homes possess WWII weapons that are strictly illegal under the strict Danish gun control laws. These unregistered and thus statistically non-existent weapons are still kept by the Danish citizenry "just in case," and during yearly amnesties hundreds of such weapons are turned over to the police.

ii ii ii

One day, Dr. Best came by in a big car chauffeured by a Resistance man. He was in civilian clothes and waved and smiled to us kids standing at the gate of his estate, Rydhave, which today is the American ambassador's home. With his very heavy black eyebrows, he was hard to miss. The Germans had looted the gold reserves in the Danish National Bank and unsubstantiated rumors had it that some of that gold had been found hidden in the handles of Dr. Best's tennis rackets.

ii ii ii

A few days after the Liberation, the British Royal Air Force held an impressive air show in Copenhagen. A large fleet of RAF planes, mainly Spitfires and Mosquitoes, flew in and bombed the hated German patrol planes that had disturbed our peace and quiet for five years. A number of the Blohm & Voss 138 three-engine flying boats were moored off Copenhagen and were destroyed by the Mosquitoes. The wreckage of one was found a couple of years ago, salvaged, and placed at the technical museum in Helsingør where its unrestorable remains are on display next to its U.S. counterpart, the Consolidated PBY Catalina. Having been there, I am sure that there certainly were more than two of the ugly things moored in the Øresund that glorious day and they all went to their just reward, courtesy of the Royal Air Force. My cousin and I had a great time as we watched the show from a fishing boat offshore.

R.A.F.'s Gloster Meteor jet fighters also participated in the show. This was the only jet that actively served in the Allied air forces during WWII and the first jet I had ever seen. Compared to the Spitfires, Mustangs, and Mosquitoes its speed—and noise—was awesome. The future had arrived!

ii ii ii

We had seen killings, bombings, and dead bodies, and were aware of what had happened to friends and acquaintances of the family at the hands of the Germans and their Danish auxiliaries.

While we knew of the horrible things—torture, reprisals, executions—that had taken place under the German occupation, however, few pictures had ever surfaced.

Although there were no death camps in Denmark and none of us lived next to any, we knew of the concentration camps in Germany and the horrible conditions that existed not only in the camps but also during the transport to them. When the flood of photographs from the concentration camps began to appear, we were overwhelmed and traumatized—especially the children. The pictures affected me a great deal, so my mother and I discussed it and I agreed for a year to have her censor all magazines before I saw them.

A different and lifelong trauma hit innocent children whose fathers or mothers had been collaborators. They would spend their lives somehow justifying the acts of their parents, even though nobody blamed the children for the sins of their fathers. Worst hit were the children of Danish mothers and mostly unknown or dead German soldiers. To this day, those children exist in a strange limbo.

Chapter 11
Aftermath

One day I came home from school and my grandfather surprised me by taking me to the local BP service station to fill up the Vauxhall with gas for the first time in five years. He had gotten his license plates back that morning and wanted to share the first ride with me! As the Germans had begun confiscating blocked-up cars, he had taken the wheels off and hidden them in my grandmother's closet, thus putting a stop to the in-and-out-of-the-garage rides that we kids had enjoyed till then.

One of the first items on the post-liberation agenda was to deal with traitors and collaborators. Professor Mogens Fog was appointed as Minister for Special Affairs in the first post-war government to head the showdown with and prosecution of the Danish traitors and collaborators. He himself had served in the Resistance and had escaped the bombing by the RAF of the Shell House.

The Danish traitors and collaborators were locked up in the former German camps and prisons. The Frøslev camp on the German border was renamed the Fårhus camp, so that the new inmates would not be confused with the patriots who had suffered imprisonment by the Germans there during the Occupation. Frøslev and Fårhus are neighboring villages next to the camp. (Since then, the camp has been very much sanitized and is discreetly open to the public. Discreetly, as nobody wants to embarrass the thousands of German tourists that today cross the nearby, unguarded border to enjoy the beaches of western Jutland.)

The death penalty was reinstated retroactively. This step of course was more than questionable constitutionally, but met no great resistance at the time. As Denmark's last hangman had died in the previous century, the new method of execution had yet to be established.

On May 5, 1945, it would have been easy to round up an impromptu firing squad on any street in Copenhagen, but by the time the sentences were imposed and appeals exhausted, tempers had cooled and it became a problem to identify who would actually carry out the death sentences and how. It was finally decided that the executions were to be handled by the police. The members of the firing squads were selected from volunteer police officers and were unknown to each other. They were placed in booths, unable to see one another, and some of the ammunition used were blanks so that no member of the firing squad would know if his shot killed the condemned criminal.

Danes who had served in the Waffen SS and had not transferred into one of the auxiliary police units in Denmark, such as HIPO, were given a fixed, reasonably short prison sentence of approximately six years. Originally the Germans had promised these Danish Waffen SS that they would not be asked to serve against the Western allies, but only to fight on the Eastern Front. The ubiquitous Danish SS recruiting posters showed a heroic SS soldier cradling a submachine gun, with the caption, "Join the SS and fight Bolshevism."

The remains of the *Freikorps Dänemark*—originally attached to the SS *Totenkopf Division* (Deathhead Division) were merged into regular Waffen SS units constituted of foreign volunteers from the occupied countries and Sweden, primarily SS Divisions *Nordland* and *Wiking*. Some of these units were the last cohesive and organized units participating in the final battle for Berlin. At that time the volunteers were keenly aware that they had to fight to the last man, as capture by the Soviets meant the firing squad and they had no home to which they could return.

In Denmark, the German leadership was placed before Danish courts and their trials went through the usual three-stage appeal process. The lower court sentenced Best and Pancke to death.

The defense appealed and the Court of Appeal imposed much lighter sentences. This caused considerable uproar among the Danish public. As there is no double jeopardy protection in Danish law, the prosecution appealed to the Supreme Court, and while neither was condemned to death, each did have to serve jail time before being deported to Germany. Werner Best was released and returned to Germany in 1951.

A separate court was set up to deal with Danish civil servants, such as my Uncle M, whose behavior seemed to indicate that they had collaborated more than absolutely necessary with the occupiers. Most sentences handed down by this court were administrative. Considering that the civil service during the period of accommodation prior to August 29, 1943, had been encouraged by the Danish government to cooperate with the Germans, many of these sentences were later quietly reversed.

ii ii ii

In Denmark, as in the rest of Europe, the signals were soon changed from war against the Germans to resistance against the Soviet expansion in Europe. The situation became especially acute after the Communist takeover of Czechoslovakia.

The Danish armed forces had to start from scratch, building on the surviving pre-war officers and non-commissioned officers and using the Swedish-equipped Danish Brigade as its new core. Some Resistance men applied for and were granted commissions in the new armed forces. All the equipment, except for what had come with the Danish Brigade from Sweden, was purchased from the British and was mostly second hand. The British troops in Denmark destroyed or confiscated whatever German equipment was still usable, all artillery pieces being spiked and rendered inoperable. In Norway, the Norwegians did not allow this to happen and built their post-war armed forces on captured German equipment, including submarines and fighter aircraft.

German soldiers under Danish command and wearing German uniforms were engaged in the removal of land mines as late as 1948, when I last saw them on the West coast of Jutland. German naval units, also under command of Danish officers, swept the minefields in Danish waters for about five years after the surrender.

In the summer of 1948 I went to Scotland to visit our relatives in Edinburgh, sailing over the North Sea on the S/S *Thyra* and returning on the S/S *Bergenhus*, both old freighters of the DFDS shipping line. The S/S *Thyra* had participated in the Normandy invasion. Her captain spent the entire trip to Scotland in his cabin, drinking. He had lost his son in the war. Both ships were refrigerated and used to ship butter to Great Britain.

On the way over we passed by the half submerged wreck of the S/S *Kjøbenhavn*. Built in 1918, she was a DFDS passenger ship that, while sailing from Copenhagen to Aalborg, hit a mine in the Kattegat.

On the way back, we saw a floating mine in the North Sea off Middlesborough in England. The belligerents usually placed their mines in predetermined minefields, moored to anchors. The anchor chains would rust through, freeing up the mines. Even if the known minefields could be swept, the floating mines continued to be a risk for a long time after the war. Every evening the newscasters on the Danish radio would announce the locations of recently observed floating mines.

ii ii ii

After the Liberation in 1945, the militant Communists went underground again, hiding their weapons and equipment in the hope and expectation of a Soviet invasion or Communist coup d'état. To protect the country against the threatening Soviet invasion, talks were held with Norway and Sweden about forming a defensive union. Eventually Denmark and Norway decided to join NATO and at that point began receiving new U.S. equipment. The U. S. funded Marshall Plan was a great help to the country and neutralized the attempts by the well organized, armed and popular Danish Communists to gain power in the country.

Even my mother voted Communist in the 1945 municipal elections, as it was the only party that had a female candidate on the ballot. As an early civics lesson, I would always accompany her to the voting booth.

The civilian population went back to work to make a living and rebuild the country. As export of Danish agricultural products, especially to Great Britain, was vital to the economic survival of the country, food rationing continued for—in some cases—five years after the war, but imported goods were slowly reappearing in the stores.

The Danish currency had been completely debased, as the country had to fund the total cost of the German occupation and the construction of the fortifications built by the Germans. It was very difficult to import anything that had to be paid for in hard currencies, i.e. U.S. Dollars, and very strict currency restrictions were imposed. You could purchase boat and plane tickets with Danish currency, but, as an example, when I left for Venezuela in 1948, I was only allowed to exchange enough Danish Kroner to purchase $25 in "spending money" for a trip half-way around the world. Soon after the Liberation all Danish currency had to be exchanged for new money. The main purpose of this exchange was to find hidden fortunes made during the war by those who did business with the Germans or earned on the black market.

If a Dane had more than a relatively small amount of money in his or her bank account, a complete accounting had to be made for the origin of these monies. My mother had about $1,000 in a savings account, the remains of a wedding present from her parents given to her some fifteen years earlier. She had to account for this money to the government.

ii ii ii

An enormous problem was caused by the nearly quarter of a million German civilian refugees in a population of 4,000,000 Danes. Many of them had been isolated in the schools that had been first requisitioned by the German military and subsequently vacated after the surrender. There, they had been kept until arrangements could be made to ship them home to Germany.

Due to their behavior toward the Danish civilians when they arrived as refugees in 1944-45, there was little tolerance towards the refugees, so they were kept mostly out of sight. They were fed, clothed, and given medical attention by the Danish government, which also established schools run by German teachers to educate the refugee children in the camps.

It took nearly four years for the refugee population to finally leave Denmark, due in large part to the fact that the Soviets were only allowing able-bodied adults to leave and return to Germany. Most of the refugees were elderly people and mothers with young children in poor health. I remember there were German refugees in the little town of Klitmøller, where we went on vacation in 1947 and 1948. There, rows of small white crosses filled the local cemetery. Most had the names of children less than a year old on them.

Another refugee and humanitarian problem was that of refugees from Estonia, Lithuania, and Latvia, as well as the Soviet prisoners of war in Denmark. If returned to the Soviet Union, the civilians from the Baltic countries were routinely either executed or sent directly to Siberia as slave laborers. While the Soviet POWs were repatriated to the Soviet Union, any of the Baltic refugees in Denmark who did not want to return to the former Baltic states were allowed to stay in Denmark and were quickly absorbed into the Danish community.

Stalin considered all Soviet soldiers who had surrendered to the Germans as traitors, so they were sent directly to Siberia on their return home. Stalin's own son was captured by the Germans who tried to make political capital of him. The Soviets refused to go along and young Stalin was "shot while trying to escape" his German POW camp.

ⵝ ⵝ ⵝ

My mother had met an old friend of the family who had spent the war years in Venezuela. He had returned for the first time since 1938 to visit his family, and attended one of my cousins' confirmation in Slagelse. There he met my mother and in the summer of 1948 she traveled to Venezuela to marry him. The original intent was for me to finish my schooling in Denmark, but Joseph Stalin intervened by starting the Berlin blockade. In Denmark it was strongly felt that this was the overture to World War III, so in October 1948 I went to Venezuela to join my mother, not to return to Denmark on vacation till fourteen years later in 1962. Fortunately World War III did not erupt, but as Rudyard Kipling said, that is another story.

ⵝ ⵝ ⵝ

In the 1960s I knew two Germans in Northford, Connecticut, who were old enough to have served as German officers. Both had been recruited and brought to the U.S. after the war by a major American corporation.

W had been an Oberleutnant, a Messerschmitt BF-109 pilot in the Luftwaffe, and U had been an officer in the Kriegsmarine. Sooner or later, and in the case of U much sooner, came the expected, albeit unsolicited and unwelcome statement, "Yes, I was in Denmark in 1944. And I loved it!" U was still a Nazi. Although his own father-in-law had been in a concentration camp for being a Social Democrat, he refused to admit that these camps had existed. He thought the Danes were a great people who had treated him wonderfully during his visit!

W told me how he and another pilot had landed in Kastrup airport in Copenhagen, and had asked a Danish farmer to lend them bicycles so they could get into town. They were pleased that he did so and they brought the bikes back on their return from the city. It obviously did not occur to W that no Dane in his right mind would have refused a German officer the "loan" of his bicycle,

For a while I also had a German boss, K. One evening he had had too much to drink—not an unusual occurrence—and he trapped me in my office for hours telling me about his experiences when he, in 1945, as a young lieutenant in the Wehrmacht, had been captured by the British. He felt that he had been badly mistreated, especially by the Dutch civilians. I, for some reason, could not work up any sympathy for him.

It was obvious that neither W, U, nor K "got it"—even twenty years later!

Epilogue

The official German lists of executed Danes contain 112 names, one of them being that of Svend Otto Nielsen.

Svend Otto Nielsen
Born: August 29, 1908
Died: April 27, 1944

Svend Otto Nielsen was born in Ashøje, Herfølge parish, son of forester Carl Peder Christian Nielsen and his wife Astrid Vilhelmine Thomsen of Hjortespring, Årestrup parish, Støvring. He was a teacher at Skovshoved School and was the brother of forester Knud Nielsen of Hjortespring by Haverslev.

Nielsen, whose nom-de-guerre was "John," carried out many incredible acts of bravery. His accomplishments on the battlefield were examples of what an army of capable and focused men who fought to protect Danish culture could do. What follows is quoted from *Politiken* and *Folkeskolen*, two Danish Newspapers.

"John entered the Resistance early and was part of the first *Holger Danske* group. He also worked closely with the British Secret Service. One evening he carried out a unique action that should have earned him a high British decoration for valor. He sneaked into Kastrup Airport to obtain information about a certain piece of equipment on the German bombers. A mechanic who was familiar with the area showed him the way, but in the middle of the air base they were discovered by the German guards. The mechanic was caught, while John hid in the dark.

"He subsequently freed the mechanic by shooting at the guards and got him out of the airport. While the Germans were busy investigating, he crept back over the fence and into a German aircraft and retrieved the device that the English wanted to know about. Later he said, 'I nearly had to dismantle the whole airplane to find the gadget. I had no idea how something like that was put together.'

"The *Holger Danske* group was by then so compromised by arrests and persecution that the group was dissolved. John became the leader of *Holger Danske II*, later known as the *Jørgen Kieler Group*. This group consisted of young people, primarily military cadets and medical students. With them John carried out the first large scale sabotage actions. Groups of only four or five men, armed with a few revolvers had been used until then. Now the scale of the actions had increased and had the character of military attacks: 20-30 men armed with submachine guns would capture the guards and then put the target enterprise out of action.

"John was caught November 9, 1943. He was betrayed by Mrs. Hedvig Delbo, in whose apartment on Fakse Street he and another man, Gunnar Dyrberg, had been living. That morning Hedvig Delbo went out to buy fresh bread. She stayed away longer than usual and when John and the other man went down to the street, Gestapo cars were waiting at each end of the block. They mounted their bicycles and rode up Nordre Frihavn Street with the cars following them. To confirm that they were being followed they reversed course at the Triangel square into Østeralle. When it was clear that the cars were indeed following them John yelled to his companion, 'Let's go!' and they stepped on the pedals. Dyrberg escaped, but John was hit when he turned the corner. He fell on the sidewalk and while lying on the ground emptied his revolver against the pursuers. They replied by repeatedly shooting the now defenseless man.

"He was thrown into the German car and driven to Dagmarhus, where he was left without receiving medical attention on a stone floor. A German physician eventually determined that he had been shot seven times in the lower parts of his body. One bullet had smashed his right femur. The physician declared that he would only live a couple of hours, so the Germans got busy interrogating him.

"To force him to talk they twisted the broken leg to one side until it was at right angles to his body. They were not able to make him talk.

"Following a short stay at the Nylands Road military hospital he was sent to Vestre prison without even being bandaged. There he was thrown on the pallet in cell No.63 where he stayed for nearly two months without receiving medical attention. He grew a full reddish-brown beard and his mattress became caked with blood, puss, and excrement. He only had his soup with which to wash himself. After many useless requests, his fellow prisoners finally were given permission to help him. Attorney S.Heltborg, who himself had been imprisoned seven months, tells us:

I will never understand how the German soldiers accepted the inhuman manner in which John was treated. He laid there, his body all shot up, his knees pulled up under his chin, paralyzed and suffering. Nobody helped him; nobody picked him up from that obscene prison pallet. He survived four months in the deepest misery, but this saboteur blessed by God, was never defeated.

Shortly before he was condemned and executed, he was granted the privilege of being carried to the toilet twice a day. Until then he had not been allowed to leave his bed. I was assigned to help him. Two men walked next to him so he could put his arms around their shoulders.

'You probably don't recognize me anymore,' he said. 'I have not seen myself in a mirror for three months and I am under the impression that I must look pretty greasy and overgrown, but what a gift to be able to go to the toilet. That is nearly as good as being pardoned.' I barely recognized John.

When last I had seen him he was the handsome and virile John who calmly and deliberately would explain his plans. He had the first rate teacher's ability to patiently explain a case so that the audience could understand him. No wonder that the students at Skovshoved School loved him.

'None of this means anything to me,' John said. 'Let them shoot me. I do not consider myself the center of the universe, even though my life right now hangs from a dirty Nazi thread. Didn't the ancient Greeks want their memories to live eternally? As for me, do not think about me.'

I talked with him again the day before he was executed. 'You know what?' he said, 'I have a really bizarre thought: If they are going to shoot me, they must do it while I am sitting in a wheelchair. Rather than an Our Father, can you give me some saying for the road? I will write it in the wind or in the running water.' The last words to me before the cell door closed were, 'A month from now you will be smiling!'

"At the beginning of April the Germans again began issuing death sentences. The point of the Nazi dagger was also pointed toward John. His letters talk of his last hours and days.

"On April 8 he writes to forester Nielsen, his brother: 'I would like to walk with you through your forest now that the leaves are coming out. It is doubtful whether I will be able to enjoy my sports and hobbies again. Right now my leg is totally useless and without an operation it will never get better. The doctor has promised me crutches and I hope to get them. It would nice for a change to be able to get up and hobble around a bit, if only I had the strength to do so.'"

"The evening of April 26th he was condemned to death and at 3 a.m. he writes his brother and sister-in-law:

"'I suppose you are wondering how come I write with ink, which is not normal, but it is a highly unusual time. Yesterday they shaved off my beautiful beard and l guessed that that meant that something was about to happen. Today they carried me to Dagmarhus, the court martial was at 8 p.m., and I was condemned to death, brought back to my cell and at 2:30 a.m. the judge came and told me that the sentence had been confirmed and was to be executed at 6 a.m. So I have three hours left to live. Till now I have taken it with a strange calm, even with a sign of a smile, God willing, I will die in the same way. I want to die with dignity. Now that it is over, I wonder if one hears the shot or is one dead before then? Well, I will soon know. I am not afraid of dying and I hope that I will not become so, but it is easy to brag early, courage has its limits...'

"The last that John wrote is dated Thursday April 27 at 4:45 a.m. He wrote to his wife and little daughter saying, '...do not mourn me, I do not want you to; be sensible, as you cannot change what has happened; I am reserved and calm. I received my sentence with a smile on my lips. Yes, one can get to be that way; these last seven months have toughened me. It is now

5 a.m. I received some excellent pieces of Smørrebrød and am enjoying my coffee with a really good old-fashioned cigar. May the Almighty let me enter death as calmly, He who has given me the strength to bear these painful months. I wish for peace in the world soon, peace in your minds, peace and good luck for our little country and my last prayer is for your future. My loving thoughts and greetings, Svend.'"

ii ii ii

Svend Otto Nielsen was faithful to his comrades-in-arms till the end. During the actions, he as the group leader was the first to attack, the last to leave the site. His comrades and the many Jews that he helped to get to Sweden have only praise for his energy, his wealth of ideas, his loyalty, his helpfulness, and his humor. He was treated especially badly, had only the Bible and some German textbooks to read, he was seldom allowed to smoke and never to receive visitors.

Fearing demonstrations, neither Dr. Best nor the infamous Bunke would allow his corpse to be turned over to the family, as he had, according to one German policeman, become a hero to the Resistance. But, according to Dr. Best, he was given a decent burial in a Danish churchyard, in a grave that could be identified in order for his corpse to be returned over to his family at a future time.

A high ranking officer of the SS Police Court admitted that he met his death bravely when he was shot by 10 German soldiers, and that he was treated with military honor, being shot rather than hung, as those who attempted to kill Hitler had been. He was able to live up to the motto that he had written in his students' poetry books:

"If you gave everything except your life. Know then that you have given nothing." -From *Fire* by Ibsen

[Adapted from Svend Schultz-Hansen from notes by Th. Johansen. Translated from the Danish by Peter H. Tveskov and used by permission.]

Bibliography & Other Sources

Barfoed, Ole. The Star of David never came to Denmark, *Politikens Kronik*, 1983.

D'Este, Carlo. *Eisenhower: A Soldier's Life*. New York, Henry Holt, 2002.

Dagbladet Politiken. *Fra Undertrykkelse Til Befrielse: 5 Aars Besættelse I billeder*. Copenhagen, J. Jørgensen & Co, 1945.

Flender, Harold. *Rescue in Denmark*. Washington D.C., United States Holocaust Memorial Museum, 1963.

Helms, Nik M. *Danmarks Historie*. Copenhagen, Gyldendal, 1943.

Higham, Charles. *Trading with the Enemy: An Exposé of the Nazi-American Money Plot, 1933-1949*. New York, Delecorte Press, 1995.

Ilsøe, Peter. *Nordens Historie*. Copenhagen, Gyldendal, 1951.

Kjersgaards, Erik. *Danmarks Historie 3: Købmand-Landmand-Arbejder*. Copenhagen, Forlaget Komma, 1982.

Lampe, David. *The Danish Resistance*. New York, Ballantine Books, 1960.

Loeffler, Martha. *Boats in the Night: Knud Dyby's Involvement in the Rescue of the Danish Jews and the Danish Resistance*. Blair, Lur Publications, 2000.

Melchior, Bent. The Salvation of the Danish Jews Forty Years Ago. *Politikens Kronik, 1983*.

Mentze, Ernst. *5 Years: The Occupation of Denmark In Pictures*. Malmö, A.B. Allhems Förlag, 1947.

Nordstrom, Byron J. *Scandinavia Since 1500*. Minneapolis, University of Minnesota Press, 2001.

Outze, Børge (editor). *Denmark During the German Occupation*. Copenhagen, The Scandinavian Publishing Company, 1955.

Shirer, William L. *The Rise and Fall of the Third Reich*. New York, Simon and Schuster, 1960.

The Challenge of Scandinavia: Norway, Sweden, Denmark, and Finland in our Time. Boston, Little, Brown, and Company, 1956.

Other Sources

Mette Grønning & Jørgen Brøndlund Nielsen, *Støvring Folkehøjskole*. Støvring, Denmark

Ebba Sellström, *Väddö Folkhögskola*. Väddö, Sweden

Eli Richardt Lindum. Copenhagen, Denmark

Axel Brygmann. Bryrup, Denmark

Printed in the United States
15631LVS00007B/151